# SWIVEL - *AGAIN*

then:
Assess. Refocus. Act. Succeed.

Design for a fast changing world
of complexity.

by
Paquita Lamacraft

*Second Edition: May 2025*

ISBN 978-1-9996273-9-3

Cover Design by Tiger Ink, Hampshire, England
Author's Web Address: www.paquitalamacraft.com
Bowyer Publishing Farnham, Surrey, England

Other books by the author:
The Cuban Approach: The art of letting go
*More* Shrapnel Free Explosive Growth
Gift Books: Quotes from a thoughtful traveller; Business quotes

# Table of Contents

# FOREWORD

In today's fast-evolving, complex world, adaptability is essential. With 40 years in financial services, I've seen how flexibility and authenticity transform challenges into opportunities. My company's success reflects this through tailored client solutions.

SWIVEL offers a practical guide for leaders and individuals to craft their solutions to thrive amid uncertainty.

This book blends strategic insight with actionable steps, from understanding "Black Swan" events to a clear process of assessment, refocusing, action, and success.

The SWIVEL framework combines big-picture vision with detailed adjustments, addressing core assets, values, people, finances, and innovation. It emphasizes values-based leadership, authenticity, and social capital in a connected world.

I've seen the author's dedication to empowering teams, and this book reflects that expertise. It's a vital resource for leaders and entrepreneurs navigating disruption, offering tools and inspiration to embrace change confidently. Dive in and apply its lessons for sustainable success.

Tony Redondo
Founder Director
Cosmos Currency Exchange Ltd
May 2025

## Authors Note: 2nd Edition

In the five years since SWIVEL was written as an immediate guide to a shut-down Covid world from which everyone would emerge to rethink to new realities, Black Swans seem to have bred. A changed world order and commanding new technologies demand an even more radical re-think.

In the course of becoming a Fellow of the Strategic Doing Institute, I contributed to my peers much of the material from the first edition of SWIVEL and from my previous book Shrapnel Free Explosive Growth. In doing so I was struck with how appropriate to new realities were many of the references and guides provided. Similarly, many were past their 'use-by date'. Second editions of both were developed accordingly, with more current additions and deletions of things no longer relevant.

The second edition of SWIVEL has one goal: provide you with examples and guidelines that will help you and your team to undertake a radical rethink of your business proposition and its current relevance, so it thrives rather than just survives.

This is not a job for AI, but in parts this technology and others can be a helpful assistants, and this we discuss.

After reading SWIVEL you will have tools to respond to this fast changing and radically different world. Never was there a more urgent task for your survival.

Paquita Lamacraft
France 13th April 2025

# INTRODUCTION
## Why 'Swivel'?

*Shall I teach you the meaning of knowledge?*
*When you know a thing, to recognise that you know it*
*and when you do not, to know that you do not know*
*– that is knowledge.*

Confucius

It is hard to encapsulate the contents of this book in one word, but 'SWIVEL' seems to do so. Why? Your former perspective needs to be refined by input from a broader view. That is why you need *everyone* to swivel. It is a daunting task and one that must be quickly and effectively done, but as you dampen mounting anxieties about the future of your company, remember the old quote:

*Sometimes the best thing about the job*
*is that the chair swivels.*

In this case that is not a frivolous statement, because unless you do **Swivel Again**, you cannot quickly assess the perspectives that have impacted and will impact your business as it existed before the impact of startling new changes to the world order and the impact of AI.

These perspectives do not lie along any familiar horizon. In his book 'Hidden in Plain Sight'[1], Erich Joachimsthalter quotes something pertinent to this that he gleaned from Alan Kay:

*Perspective is worth 50 IQ points.*

Alan Kay should know about perspective. He is a Fellow of the American Academy of Arts and Sciences, the National Academy of Engineering, *and* the Royal Society of the Arts and amongst other things he invented is the GUI interface - pronounced "gooey".

The GUI (graphical user interface) lets all the bits attached to the computer and the software within it talk to each other happily (when well designed). Kay was also a professional jazz musician, composer and theatrical designer, so has wider than average perspective.  His wide range of interests is a frequent mix for those who alert us to crossover opportunities and potential relationships otherwise invisible.

Why is perspective so important? Nassim Nicholas Taleb reminds us in 'Fooled by Randomness'[2], that *bad information is worse than no information at all.*

Bad information can also be labelled otherwise as 'assumptions', 'expectations', 'someone told me that's the way it happens', 'everything is operating smoothly'

---

[1] Hidden in Plain Sight, Erich Joachimsthalter - My version printed in 2007
[2] Fooled by Randomness, Nassim Nicholas Taleb - My version printed in 2005

and – 'Oh no. That was just a one-off problem'. In more current times it can include creative hallucinations of your AI tool, or the fact that the inputs to the AI that you are using should always be qualified by people – male and female – and so should the outputs. As AI tilts to North America, specifically include in the way you frame an enquiry the named countries in which you operate, or that perspective will be lost to you.

This is because much of what was input into the large language models from which AI draws its outputs predominantly reflects the output of white male North Americans. Or, from inputs described by Gerd Gigerenzer in 'The Intelligence of Intuition'[3] as WEIRD: **W**estern, **E**ducated, **I**ndustrialised, **R**ich, and **D**emocratic – which represents about 12% of the world's population. If you add to that the extensive data bias in a world designed for men, as documented in 'Invisible Women'[4] by Caroline Criado Perez, the need for 'sense-checking' with a critical eye and thoughtful assessment cannot be more widely emphasised.

You need to benefit from the diverse thinking of your own people to add value and critical thought to the AI outputs. AI aficionados will challenge that statement, assuring you that AI algorithms capture "everything". It is rather like your backup of your IT system. It backs up "everything" as long as "everything" is in the places it looks for them.

---

[3] The Intelligence of Intuition, Gerd Gigerenzer – My version printed in 2023
[4] Invisible Women, Caroline Criado Perez – My version printed in 2019

SWIVEL

For use of AI, GDPR compliance is important. Define and record specific, detailed uses you make of AI, and follow the rules for Data Protection Impact Assessments as outlined in Article 35 [5]of the Act – or your company may be the one with bad information.

If you use AI to produce synthetic data (generated rather than obtained from observing real world), be aware of those dangers also, especially if used for decision-making. This is well worth researching. Just be aware that this takes up massive memory and although you created it, you still have to keep it, show how it was created and used, and have all this audited.

One of the worst pieces of bad information might be something you are prone to yourself, and that is miscalculating what is making your business profitable. When your *Swivel* rests in the area of profit, the way you measure profit may be altering your perspective on the reality of your finances, something we will examine as we swivel together.

When you *Swivel* you and your team will be able to check for yourselves what things look like from every angle: so swivel - but not alone. *Swivel* in a joint effort with your existing staff. Where their chairs are situated gives different perspectives from where you sit, and from those of each other.

---

[5] https://gdpr-info.eu/art-35-gdpr/

In 'Hope Is Not A Method'[6], written by the General who had the tasked of making the modern US Army fit for this era and not the last, authors Gordon. R. Sullivan (General) and his colleague Michael V. Harper (Colonel) write that leadership is about unleashing the power of the people – and that expectations are 'best established in dialogue'. They also value the ***Swivel*** because, as they say:...*peripheral vision is unfortunately as rare in crisis as in good times.*

Empowering participation of the whole organisation is echoed in 'Cognitive Surplus: Creativity and Generosity in a Connected Age'[7]. In this book, author Clay Shirky points out that the need for a term called 'participatory culture' is a 20th century need. Prior to that it would have been what is called a 'tautology' – a phrase or expression that means the same thing said twice in different words – because before the 20th century culture *was* participatory. He makes a point we should consider. To 'participate' is to feel as if your presence matters. If you invite participation ensure that everyone feels that his or her presence matters. It does. You need contributions from everyone as you swivel.

***Swivel*** to:
- Take stock of where you are and the implications of new realities.
- Recognise where opportunity lies.
- Prioritise, and act.

---

6 Hope is Not a Method, Gordon. R. Sullivan and Michael V. Harper - My version printed in 1996
7 Cognitive Surplus, Clay Shirky - My version printed in 2011

Without that joint level of survey – a 360° survey - you cannot be well-enough informed to:

## ASSESS
- Make a health assessment of how well your business is coping under rapidly shifting constraints and identify areas for improvement.
- Spot where there are hazards ahead – either clear on the horizon, or merely indicated by the tip of an iceberg.
- Undertake a small team's challenge to creatively destroy and reassemble or recreate each aspect of your value proposition or of every product you sell.
- At the same time identify the emerging gaps and opportunities in the market you serve and isolate which parts of your existing business offer new market openings you never saw before.
- Identify the known impacts from new technologies or market realities
- Map your 'holding pattern' and know what it should incorporate as you assess and then plan the route forward.

## REFOCUS
- Review results of the assessment of your products and services. What does it reveal? Where are you vulnerable and why? What new 'reassemble' or 'destruction;' makes sense to explore further?
- Reaffirm your business core product or service and be honest about its suitability to address the original problem it was developed to solve – or grasp quickly a new, more sustaining focus to use your unique assets to solve something even more common or urgent (or both) in current times.
- Map all your current assets
- Link and leverage all your assets

- Make a list of areas where external collaboration makes sense.
- Define the logical essential pathways forward.
- With your staff work out what people with what skills need to be deployed where and to what purpose.
- Re-evaluate finance.

## ACT

- Communicate your holding pattern and/or your new flight path effectively to your own team and to those with whom you have broader business relationships.
- Refocus financial commitments, sources of funds, and priority spend.
- Keep the business running while you develop new options.
- Create an organisational structure fit for new purposes.
- Reassign existing staff, or assist them to redeploy elsewhere.
- Rebrand - or just polish your brand to tell the world what your newly focused core business is - and why it matters.
- Build on, and broadcast your values.
- Keep perspective and have some fun together, despite the pressing need for outcomes.

## SUCCEED

- Aim for small early victories. Make small steps fast instead of big steps slowly. Test and iterate.
- Tweak the plan as needed -do not shift focus from your plan without good reason.
- By regularly checking progress with your teams, correct errors of early judgement before they become impediments to success.

- Develop an agreed regular 'huddle' to respond to the emergence of new winds of opportunity or looming storm clouds.
- Pay back: reward your own people and give some support to the communities where you work and the helping organisations within it.

*Nothing so powerfully concentrates a man's mind as to know that he will be hung in the morning.*
Dr. Johnson

You are not likely to be hung in the morning, but unless your assessment is quick and comprehensive and leads to a total re-evaluation of your company's future – it may not have one – or at least not the one you would prefer.

What will we have to consider? You will need to make a status check that is totally objective, showing the impact of current global realities on your current business health. A great place to start is to actually get out there and talk to your customers. You. Not a team. You.

The impression this has on the customer cannot be underestimated and ten such visits will give you a random snapshot of information you would never otherwise have known or considered. It is also the basis of deciding together what makes sense to do together in the face of these challenges. Afterwards:

- Identify whether you can still supply as before the same goods and/or services at the same quality, speed and cost, and by the same methods. If not-how, and what are the alternatives?

# SWIVEL

- Identify 'Wobble Points' and 'Building Blocks'. You need to be operational even while you SWIVEL and you may need to patch and fence-mend to do so.
- Clearly check the validity of past assumptions and expectations against current realities
- Make a critical evaluation of the value proposition of your company. Does it still make sense or have new realities impacted that, making alternative directions become realistic so you can capture new opportunities?
- Define what success will look like.
- Assign responsibilities AND tasks – they are not the same thing.
- Review objectively the relevance of what you previously supplied and what is now most required/desired/irrelevant - from your business and your supply chain and fulfillment teams.
- Create a timeline that is unforgiving and a measurement of progress that is simple and effective.
- Communicate: to your own people, your existing supply chain, your fulfillment people, and your existing clients.
- Review organisational structure to be fit for purpose.
- Refine and delete as many as possible of all your processes and approvals – giving more autonomy.
- Seek out new opportunities and be realistic about the pathway to seizing them – and the cost and timeframe necessary to be successful – and how these will have impact on current business, and how that will be managed.
- Map how to sustain 'business as it was' against 'business as it will need to be' and show how the transition will be made – and by when, and at what cost, and with whose involvement.

# SWIVEL

A friend of mine gave me a great hint that I now employ when starting something new. It is a simple thing but it does work. Before starting a new project, clear your desk and polish it. Clear everything off, clean it, and put things back. This not only clears the physical space for action, it refreshes your mind by also clearing out the debris of thoughts that have no bearing on the task at hand. Then, your starting point is to **Swivel**.

When you do, remember something that Edward de Bono points out in his book 'Innovation and Entrepreneurship': that
>*when we have a change in perception,*
>*it is not that the facts changed*
>*– it is just that their meaning has changed.*

Keep notes on past perceptions and how reality now has changed meaning. Changing perspective is a 'must'. So is re-evaluating meaning that was once held as constant. If you think you are looking in a 'normal' perspective as you survey the fitness and survivability of your business in this radically changed world, here is a tongue-in-cheek reality check, courtesy of Douglas Adams. In 'The Salmon of Doubt: Hitchhiking the Galaxy One Last Time' we have an indication of why what we think of as 'normal' – or used to think of as 'normal' – is only a matter of perspective.

*The fact that we live at the bottom of a deep gravity well,*
*on the surface of a gas covered planet*
*going around a nuclear fireball 90 million miles away*
*and think this to be normal is obviously some indication*
*of how skewed our perspective tends to be.*

# CHAPTER ONE
# When the Black Swan's eggs hatch

*One is never afraid of the unknown;*
*one is afraid of the known coming to an end.*

Krishnamurti

## What is a black swan
## and why is it a useful analogy?

A black swan is something that was never thought to exist because we knew all swans were white – because all the swans we had previously known about **were** white until someone travelled to Western Australia - and found *black* swans.

The Covid-19 Virus was not exactly a Black Swan. Covid-19 was the sort of threat that had been postulated by people whose job it is to anticipate threats of potentially global impact. They may not have had the feather details exactly correct but within this community evidence seemed to have been growing that there was a real possibility – or even probability – that such a creature may not yet exist – but given current assessments of likely breeding grounds, could suddenly emerge.

The fact that the bearers of such tidings were not well received is now academic.

The world was unprepared for that black swan. That is history now.

But what lessons did we learn? If we had done nothing to prepare for the arrival of the Covid black swan, it's appearance and impact should have alerted us to prepare our organisations for what may happen when we emerged into a world fragmented at places we could not fully anticipate or comprehend.

If a global pandemic didn't teach us to act to make our organisations flexible and adaptive by giving our teams more autonomy, then the radical shift in world order of the first few months of 2025 may have more impact than if we had done so.

In his book 'The Black Swan[8]', Nassim Nicholas Taleb gives such an event three values: rarity, extreme impact and after-the-fact predictability The radical shift in world order that began early in 2025 falls into the same category.

The playbook had already been written and openly declared. The fact that many businesses (and individuals) chose to ignore the implications of this being enacted and not model the "What if?s" was a choice. It may now appear that it was a very expensive one as these impacts threaten the survival of so many businesses.

Perhaps we could not have described fully what is unfolding globally at the time of writing, but had we

---

[8] The Black Swan, Nassim Nicholas Taleb – My version printed in 2007

accepted that Black Swans exist, we could have set in place structures within our organisations and our lives, so that when they did – as most assuredly they would – and in the future will – we had the bamboo scaffolding around which to clamber as we secured the supports that keep things in place.

The need for the capacity to cope with Black Swans has been well stated before. In a Alvin Toffler's 'The Adaptive Organisation'[9], there is a reprint from a report from AT&T that illustrates this. I have changed the references to 'AT&T' to be 'the organisation' as I believe they can be more generally applied.

*Many of (the organisation's) most pressing problems arise from radical changes in the external environment of the company, and the difficulties of predicting or coping with these changes at the high speed required.*

So, having accepted that Black Swans seem to be hatching at an alarming rate for an organisation designed for a different era, we should spare no time in moving forward to make our companies swan-proof.

**Does history help us plan today?**
**– and if not, what can?**

In 'The Adaptive Corporation', Toffler asks an important question that may influence how we look at the past – particularly in terms of trying to learn from it for a future that is unpredictable and unexpected.

---

[9] The Adaptive Organisation, Alvin Toffler - My version inherited from my Dad's library - printed in 1985

# SWIVEL

*Can any corporation remain truly adaptive
if it is still operating on yesterday's beliefs?*

There is no way to have plans to anticipate the unimaginable, so the only remedy is to have an organisation that has developed Black Swan Immunity – which is what we are doing with our ***Swivel***.

There is no 'playbook' for the enormity of what we face. If relevant responses in history can only give a few pointers and some of these may not even be applicable to today's reality, where else to look for guidance? In seeking the answer to that question I did what I always do when approaching something about which I know very little, but knowledge of which is crucial to an outcome: READ.

History may not give us as many clues as we wish, but many business writers of the past and present and others describing ways to address radical change have made points that can be useful to us as we survey the newly defined horizon that faces us and plan accordingly .

In Tom Peters 'classic 'Thriving on Chaos[10]', he quotes Andrea Sagu in 'Submerged Industry':

*Today, only a small, motivated firm with...
highly qualified labor and good vertical mobility
instead of oppressive hierarchy
can hold up in a world
whose principal characteristic is instability.*

---

[10] Thriving on Chaos, Tom Peters - My copy printed in 1987

# SWIVEL

I repeat. Written in 1987.

My father was a strategist: initially in the military and during deployment in wartime situations often behind enemy lines – a place where strategy meant eliminating as much risk as possible to other people's lives – in his case, his own forces and small communities of civilian locals.

Later, many lessons learned in that hard training ground were applied in his consulting with corporations, companies of all sizes, social organisations, and governments. Working with leaders and their teams on how to deal with radical change, he made it a focus to guide them to think forward in a way that 'fit' with their individual ethos and that thus drew from their strengths.

From this same basis of turning to the knowledge within your own organisations I add pointers from more than 63 books from my own library and that inherited from my father. I have read and re-read them to offer guidance and thought provocation as you face this current daunting, but essential re-assessment of your business so it can thrive in a radically changed world. To these I add references from current publications and online information and webinars.

From the books I have extracted some of the salient points I had highlighted at first reading – and many new ones I found. In some of my inherited books, the highlighting of my Dad was extremely useful. The list of all these books and other publications is in the Appendix.

Fortunately, 'reading and comprehension' is a skill I have honed; starting from the years spent doing an English/French degree where this ability was essential. I remember in one year having to report on 27 books, of which one was 'War and Peace'.

Little did I realise how useful this skill would prove later in business. ***Swivel Again*** distils the knowledge within all these books that are friends of mine and who sit close by me in my countryside office in France.

This distillation is offered  in the hope that it will inspire you, guide you, and help you pick your way through the unusual rearrangements  you find when you assess your current state of business in this new reality.

This guide does not pretend to foresee what impacts we may have to face in a global business environment that will be battered by impacts of tariffs and changed inter-country trust relationships.

The Covid-19 era flight from Treasury Bonds was illustrative of a wider issue. People didn't respond as expected. Government bonds were once the place people fled *to* in crisis – not *from*.

Now, at the time of writing in April 2025, the US Government Bond's status as the world's safest assert has been badly eroded. We do not yet know the implications of this and other damaged trust relationships, but now is the time for you to urgently solidify yours.

SWIVEL

We can have no certainty about the makeup of the world.  What we can do is isolate immediate steps that take us forward intact and productively - and make ourselves resilient for what comes next.

We can also stand out for developing a trust relationship ourselves: trust within the organisation and trust extending throughout our value chain and the communities where we operate.

The Edelman Trust Barometer Global Report of 2025 reveals a drop of trust in the employee, employer relationship and label it as 'unprecedented'. It also shows a global belief that leaders lie to us. This is at an all-time high, and it responds to a question about whether leaders purposely mislead people by 'saying things they know are false or gross exaggerations'.

This change is up 11 points for governments and the media, and even higher for business leaders - 12 points higher. Combine this with a double increase in 15 out of 18 surveyed countries when asked whether they worry about experiencing prejudice, discrimination, or racism. When asked about their own CEO, the trust level was down by 21 points.

The good news as you evaluate the environment where your business operates?

There is a 19 point increase in how ethical business is seen to be, when compared with the last report. There is also a notable desire for re-skilling existing employees to be competitive and to 'nurture workplace civility'. So, in the last positives you are already well-placed, as you wouldn't be reading this book otherwise. Overall, according to this survey, business is the most trusted institution. We should live up to that trust as we Swivel.

**It is not *intelligence* per se – it is *attitude* that will find the solution.**

Polish your attitude and get ready to ***Swivel***.

Not a bad place to start is to use something like the template used by the United Nations Office for Disaster Risk Reduction (UNDRR)[11]. This documents the 'forensic learning' from specific disasters' in the following template

---

[11] UNDRR – Global Assessment Report on Disaster Risk reduction 2024
https://www.undrr.org/media/100220/download?startDownload=20250420

|  | People | Planet | Prosperity |
|---|---|---|---|
| **Learning from the past** | What has been established that worked better this time? | What effects did damage to the environment contribute? | What economic recovery mechanisms that worked before were effective this time? |
| **Resilient features** | What are the resilient and non-resilient features of your environment? | How is the environment and geographical location of your services responding to external risk? | How evenly was the economic impact spread the organisation? |
| **To inform the future** | What are the three vital things that evaluating past events cause you to be aware of and respond to? | How well are you integrated into the overall risk profile of your community or the communities where you operate? | What can you do with the way you are now structured to minimise extensive impact from external events? |

# SWIVEL

Strategies don't have to be grand to be effective: Don Schafer had a handwritten sign on his wall. On it he wrote the city's strategy in black felt tip pen:

| | |
|---|---|
| #1 | People |
| #2 | Do it Now |
| #3 | Do it right the first time |
| #4 | Do it within budget |
| #5 | Would you like to live there? |

Who was Don Schafer? Four times elected Baltimore city Mayor: each time with more than 85% of the vote.

Schafer faced chaotic change. He was there during the closures of Bethlehem Steel, at the time the largest waterfront steel mill in the world, and also closure of the 70 year old GM auto/truck assembly plant. He saw the departure of the local American Football team 'The Colts' to Indianapolis, and the 'Bullets' basketball team to Maryland and eventually Washington.

Reviewing the assets at hand, Schafer focused on waterfront tourism. Previous mayors had developed the concept. Mayor Schafer got it done, transforming a deteriorating city into a hub of national tourism.

Although he memorably appointed Bishop L. Robinson as the city's first black Police Commissioner to give more representation to the large black community and developed a substantial community fund for small local projects (to which he passed his estate when he died), in his later role as Governor, Schafer was demonstrably sexist and claimed HIV was 'brought on people by themselves'.

# SWIVEL

*This demonstrates that Brand Value is not static.
What this man accomplished in one role was almost
effaced by his attitudes in the next.*

Like every brand, you should be aware of what yours is
saying about you: it will reflect upon those you lead.

In our work guiding business responses to the complex
challenges impacting our clients, I have always intuitively
used the methods I have now refined as in becoming a
Fellow of The Strategic Doing Institute.

In short, these include realising there are many
alternative pathways forward, but only if the new
destination has been clearly defined by those whom it
affects, and you look both ways before making a turn from
your current path.  Then it's a case of:

- Harnessing all the assets – hidden and obvious -
  within your environment and your people to link
  and leverage  the 'what have we got' assets to
  shorten the path to that goal
- Going forward with a disciplined regular learning
  loop to develop iteratively, making small mistakes
  en route so we don't make bigger ones later.

All of these skills we'll practice as we Swivel.

*Remember the expectation of  a post-Covid 'New normal'?
Normal cannot be new - or it wouldn't be normal.*

Forget 'Business as usual'. Forget 'new normal'.

'Normal' suggests things familiar. Our world has been irreparable altered - and perhaps for many of us –our values and our priorities in life have also changed, one hopes for the better.  As changes in the financial world start to impact our communities, these priorities will need reassessment.

A thought leadership paper on New Realities of Globalization from Arizona State University[12] gave a powerful message :

*Become comfortable with feeling uncomfortable.*

The Covid-19 crisis writ large the existing inequities to which we have been unaware. It exposed realities that were either invisible from our previous perspective, or known but ignored because of where we placed value. This shaking of our perception of reality has only increased with unfolding global events since.

One example was during Covid on an OECD (Organisation for Economic Co-operation and Development) Zoom call on 7th May 2020 when we learned that – much to the surprise (even amazement) of the Italian researchers in Tocino, Italy –they found that 42% of all Italian households do not have a computer.

As you see – such things are all a matter of perspective. Why didn't we know that?

---

[12] Thunderbird School of Global Management: insights/new-realities-globalization

The question was never before thought relevant, as it didn't impact on the way we organised our businesses, our lives, our efforts to encourage local and regional economic development (although here we probably missed a trick)– so it wasn't asked.

There are myriad other similar startling revelations of inequity that are not what we expected – even of lifestyle choices that create what we think to be inequities.

Of course, perhaps we should not have been so surprised about the level of personal computers in Italian households, after all, the Slow Cities Campaign started in Italy.

The way Slow Cities started was this: In 1999, Paolo Saturnini, the then mayor of the small town of Greve, in Chianti, Tuscany *(cheers Paolo- we raise a glass),* inspired a new perspective to develop the local economy. This new way was based on the valuing of a slower way of life.  The idea had (and has)  resonance beyond his city and beyond his country, and it soon spread - now in 2025 there are 305 member cities[13] in 33 geographic areas working on the same value of 'Slow' as the key development criteria.

 The Slow Cities movement has at its base respect for the progress of the seasons and the produce and pleasures these bring; authenticity - in all aspects of culture and craft; value and care of inspiring landscapes and places; in looking after the full range of the community and its needs;

---

[13] https://www.cittaslow.org/membership

and generally respecting and protecting a choice for a slower life as we plan and develop.

We find ourselves at the time of writing in April 2025, in a changed world order that happened in less than three months. The changes that have been wrought impact every nation and every level of our populations.

Even if *your* business can sustain itself in its original format (and that would be most unusual for any well-run business, given this type of change), the former structure of your supply chain, your advisory services, your markets, and the customers within them, may not. Worse, they may – but no longer be 'fit for purpose' for the new business you must create – for you must create new, or suffer –even if new means refining what was adequate in the past.

In this unfamiliar environment, all thought and guidance is to be considered on its merit – for we cannot face this sudden myriad variety of challenges with lone wisdom.

*Our best thoughts come from others.*
Ralph Waldo Emerson

**What does this book offer?**
Within these pages the methods of a variety of models have been contributed valuable input. From these you may find things to adapt or adopt as seems relevant as you come to understand the challenges you will face.

All of these models or ideas or specific guidance documents are drawn from different industry sectors, from the professions, from research, from science, from nature, from creative thinkers, and from diverse geographies. The writings span decades and also include the wisdom of the ancients.

The aim is to prompt new types of thinking – to get you to **Swivel** so that you take information from all around you – a full 360° to help you **Assess** comprehensively. The effectiveness of the range of that swivel and the assessment you make from what you learn will be the basis for you to **Refocus** to plan a future where you **Succeed**, no matter what the future throws at you.

To succeed you must **Act -** but first prioritise actions, communicate them effectively – both internally and to the outside world – be decisive, engage those who can help – and whom you can help – and stay your course. You must move from "What could we do?", through "What should we do?", to "What *will* we do?" – and then DO – quickly and effectively.

In the process, you must be building the relevant supporting structures that will give your company the flexibility to respond effectively to each unexpected turn of this big adventure we all will share.

That might mean changing existing methods, rules, or hierarchies. It may mean scrapping them and starting with something that will be best suited to the sleeker company you will design. At the very least, your changes should at least form a protective shield against the sort of impact caused by this crisis, and those which we cannot predict, but will come.

# SWIVEL

After you **Swivel** you will be in a position to enact different plans to refine and enhance what you do. Without this assessment and refocus, you would be struggling.

It is not just a case of finding ways to support the particular value you provided to a world that no longer exists in the format it did before our familiar world suddenly changed.

Your future company must be capable of responding to each new situation, and resilient enough to be flexible and *capitalise* on all future changes that come, for come they surely will. To do so, I recommend you build a structure using what I call bamboo scaffolding. Bamboo scaffolding is explained in my book 'Shrapnel Free Explosive Growth', which guides leaders to build the underpinning structure for a future company when it is growing so fast they haven't time to do it.

Bamboo is used in cyclone areas because it will flex with the raging winds – and if it comes loose is a lot less dangerous a weapon that a piece of galvanised pipe. For those of you who saw the news reporting of the April 2025 Myanmar earthquake that caused the collapse of the building that was under construction in Thailand, you could hear the metal pipes of the scaffolding hitting the ground: terrifying projectiles.

Collapse of your scaffolding would not have quite that impact but let's not even risk that and instead use bamboo. Bamboo is the analogy I use because your supporting structure needs to be flexible enough to flex in the winds of change, not self-destruct, and definitely no become a weapon itself. Then it will allow you to scramble safely around it and take in the perspectives from every angle.

*Swivel* is designed to help interpret the new vistas as you swing through 360°- and guide you through your assessment of the relevance of what you discover.

*Swivel* is not a foolproof guide. It is not a proven method. It is what the moment calls for:  a gathering of useful stories and suggestions for you to place in your kaleidoscope so that you can twist the viewing-end to see new patterns – unlikely patterns – fragmented patterns – that might inspire you with equally unforeseen indications of where your company future lies.

Rewards will be to the swift and well organised.
    You cannot afford to fail.
        There is little time to ponder.

There is little time to engage professional advisors. Worse, if you do, they have no more idea than you do about how to structure your business: the people who do are you and your business team.

This is the time, more than ever, for you to empower your own team to deal with the impact of each of the Black Swan's hatching eggs.  You will need to review the status of the body of water where you are currently nesting as well as the habitat of the wider world where your emerging birds will have to survive.

**We are all in this together**

In the UK, in response to Covid-19 there was a very important central government message, endorsed in the broadcast to the nation and the Commonwealth by Her Majesty Queen Elizabeth II, and it is one which should be your guiding principle because it has so many implications and potential ramifications. That message is:

### *We are all in this together*.

Hold that thought as you emerge. Make it central to your design for the path forward.

*We are in it together* with every level of our own business – with our supply chain and our fulfillment people.

*We are in it together* with our customers and their customers and their teams.

*We are in it together* with bureaucracy and policy-makers.

*We are in it together* with the whole education system from which we draw our talent.

*We are in it together* with our staff and their families, and those of our associates, and we are in it together with the communities where we operate.

*We are in it together* to solve some of the really big challenges ahead – and this might mean that we cross from the familiar to new territories.

We now need to work collaboratively. In the challenges ahead we may find our expertise being applied to developing solutions quite different from those that which previously used our skills, expertise, and ideas.

We are facing the "We don't know how to do" problems of a complex and fast changing world. Our businesses have been designed to effectively address the "We know how to do" problems.

We are in an Apollo 13 world. We need to clearly state the problems we face and then review what we have available to deploy a solution – and do it fast before the oxygen runs out. That's why we need to SWIVEL first.

In the book 'Strategic Doing' (Foreword by Yo-Yo Ma) Ed Morrison and his colleagues at the Agile Strategy Lab at Purdue University outlined the ten skills that were used in some remarkable cases of addressing 'don't know how to do' challenges.

These have been refined into a very useful methodology of working collaboratively with people we don't know and where no one can tell anyone else what to do. It moves from a quickly built trust environment through to doing in a disciplined set of stages on a very fast track and case studies demonstrate pivotal results from disciplined empowerment. In the words of one reviewer[14] : These are 'simple, low-cost, and low risk ways of getting the right things to happen quickly. These rules are listed at the back

---

[14] Emeritus Professor Michael Heffernan, University of the Sunshine Coast,

of this book and you will recognise their importance after working through the wider suggestions of *SWIVEL Again.*

## Implications of economic contraction

In 'The Next Economy[15], author Paul Hawken was talking about the future 'Informative Economy' while others were focusing on the technology changes themselves – technology changes we have taken for granted in our current world. Those changes also caused contraction but not at a global-all-at-once level such as we now face.

In that book Hawken makes the point that contraction *"makes consumers smarter and businesses leaner"* – and that in this new *Informative* economy practically every product or service will need to be redefined and redesigned. That was in 1983. This also applies to our current situation and it is interesting to consider his stated belief that applied at the time of his writing– and I suggest, also now:

*Remaking our world is not only our task,*
*it is probably the greatest economic opportunity*
*that has ever existed.*

There is merit in applying this thought today – but there is a singular difference of context.

When the world was locked away in its homes during Covid, those so isolated had a rare chance to evaluate the values that matter. In that period, with the time to do so and a suddenly changed perspective on 'value', how governments, companies, organisations, sporting teams,

---

[15] The Next Economy, Paul Hawkin - My copy published in 1983

interest groups, and individuals behaved was measured against the common good. It was measured against the values that have never gone out of style: honesty, kindness, generosity, fairness, and value based on activity, not on title or social status.

Post-Covid, and now with rapidly changing geo-political relationships, we have seen customer power in boycotts of brands and countries who don't honour these values. This is now playing out in purchasing choices influenced by tariffs and in 'deals' that betray ethics that have been done at high levels.

The influence has been bottom up. Mom and Pop choose not to buy from countries or organisations whose values don't align with theirs. Companies and those with high-value financial assets choose to no longer trust the future advice of the service companies who betrayed their stated ethics by making deals in high places. For many, it is their only way to object to what are seen to be unjust acts to which their governments choose not to respond.

The only way for your business to differentiate is to stand for your own values and remake your business based upon them. How this will play out as economies suffer the impacts of the geopolitical changes tilting our world to new axes is unknown. It is still worth consideration when making your forward plans.

**Are you an Adaptor or a Shaper?**

In 'The Lexus and the Olive Tree'[16], written by Thomas Friedman, the author was again talking about a *"wired world without walls'"* when he coined the two terms of 'Adaptor' and 'Shaper'. Decide which your company is - and consider the implications.

*Adaptors* don't just mould themselves to the frameworks within which they have to work, but identify and develop niche markets within them.

*Shapers* must attract a lot of adaptors to their own standard of business to become more effective themselves, but in doing so create value for others as well as their own organisation. Whichever you are, or even if you are both, you also need to be a *'Learner'.*

In 'The Anatomy of Change'[17], author Don Fabun quotes Eric Hoffer, the American social commentator who, when writing about the role of the 'under-classes', said they were "lumpy with talent". Hoffer wrote:

*In times of drastic change it is the **learners** who inherit the future. The **learned** usually find themselves equipped to live in a world that no longer exists.*

Adapt your 'Adaptor' or 'Shaper' status according to what you learn from your assessment – especially what you learn from your 'Wobble Points' and your 'Building Blocks'

---

[16] The Lexus and the Oliive Tree, Thomas Friedman - My version published in 2000
[17] The Anatomy of Change, Eric Hoffer - My version printed in 1967 and inherited from my Dad's library

(two terms of assessment we shall explore later0, and from your collective 360° *Swivel.*

## Collaboration

This brings us to the subject of collaboration, because you may learn an awful lot of useful things from collaboration with those you formerly thought of as competitors. These are often those companies to which *you* could add some value, with your own talented workforce.

Friedman introduces us to the efforts of James D. Wolfensohn, at the time President of The World Bank, who in 1999 laid out the 'Comprehensive Development Framework' for Aid.
Accordingly, I went to the website and extracted three salient points:

Collaboration makes sense when it:
- is in line with the organisation's priorities
- places no further burden on the needed in-house work obligations without obvious return-on-investment
- can be predominantly funded from within existing resources.

Think widely on collaboration. It is not all B2B that makes sense. Sometimes collaboration across different genres has big paybacks.

As we plan for our business survival and for the survival of the things that matter in this world of changed value priorities – we must give some thought to how we can help in a practical way those who make our lives worth living by the music they make, the art they create, and the valuable crafts and artisan skills that they sustain over generations.

When I was guiding the development of the Music and Film Strategy for New Orleans in 2001, HD TV was new. The artists of New Orleans wanted to learn but didn't have the resources. However, there were the following possible collaborative partners to whom it would make sense to have High Defintion skill base on which to call, rather than having it on the payroll:

- Hospitals with (pardon the pun) cutting edge surgical procedures wanting to develop training films
- Petrochemical industry to be able to interrogate feedback from probes into places and pipelines in awkward places, or stress indications on critical equipment
- Advanced shipbuilding technologies of the marine industry and the School of Naval Architecture.

By making this case I was able to approach AVID who make state-of-the-art mixing decks: they lent us one for 18 months. I think you can also see the benefit of New Orleans artists championing your product.

Collaboration with your competitors may be the solution to forging new opportunities, individually and collectively.  It makes sense.

In my book 'Shrapnel Free Explosive Growth' I cite Comité Colbert - a collaborative association that brings together 95  of the most important French companies from the luxury goods sector  to work together on things important to them all. It was started in 1954 by the designer Jean-Jacques Guerlain with the intent to promote the luxury goods of France. Now, over 86% of their goods are exported.

   This method of joining synergistic companies in the sector for a greater outcome than can be realised alone has been emulated by other similar collaborative efforts across Europe: Altagamma (Italy) Circulo Fortuny (Spain), Meisterkreis (Germany, and Walpole (England) – collectively representing over 600 brands, many of which are SMEs. Further, it is important to note that it is profitable.

*Comité Colbert businesses*
*have expanded fivefold through collaboration.*

   In 'The Creative Corporation'[18],  author Karl Albrecht contrasts the effects of 'turf wars' and other ailments of what he calls a 'stagnant' company with the results that synergy can bring. He writes:

*Synergy means cooperation, collaboration, and the*
*effective interplay of resources...*
*It is shared goals, shared stake in the outcome,*
*and shared responsibility for finding solutions.*

*Synergy is alignment.*

---

[18] The Creative Corporation, Karl Albrecht - My version printed in 1979

Industry clusters are a great place to align yourself to those with whom your company has synergy.

Find out what Industry Sector Clusters are in your region and explore connections with them. Collectively, you have a better opportunity to develop the most useful and 'sticky' responses for a rapidly changing world.

In the words of Seth Godin, author of This is Marketing[19]:

*No one is as smart as all of us.*

If you don't know where to start, in the links below there is a map with details of those globally that have affiliation with The Competitiveness Institute[20], plus the EU European cluster map[21], and US Cluster Mapping[22].

Like others who lead the development of sector-wide strategies, I am continually amazed at levels of trust that can be built, and with what speed. In these cluster groups, leaders of fiercely competitive companies come together to decide where it makes sense to collaborate.

The focus is to identify specific outcomes that have wide benefit to all. Such bonds of trust come from a common focus that from the outset recognises that there must be benefit to all who contribute or they cannot afford to invest the time to collaborate.

---

[19] This is Marketing, Seth Godin
[20] https://www.tci-network.org/members/
[21]
https://ec.europa.eu/growth/industry/policy/cluster/observatory_en
[22] http://clustermapping.us/cluster

Sometimes there are exceptions to this, for example when collaboration is forged by a wider social emergency, such as happened around the world where companies responded to the urgent and critical local needs that suddenly emerged during the pandemic.

One example is the F1 response to Covid-19 with 'Project Pitlane': a consortium of seven F1 teams : *Aston Martin Red Bull Racing, BWT Racing Point F1 Team, Haas F1 Team, McLaren F1 Team, Mercedes-AMG Petronas F1 Team, Renault DP World F1 Team, ROKiT Williams Racing.*

Project Pitlane was a collaboration of resources and capabilities that support each of the teams of F1. This collective toolbox of abilities and experience includes the capacity for rapid design, prototype manufacture, test, and of skilled, error-free rapid assembly. The participants know their core strengths and were quick to identify their applicability to development of urgently needed life-saving equipment for use in front-line medical care of those suffering from the Covid-19 virus.

F1 and its supply chain is an exemplar of response to engineering challenges under intense pressure. It is in their DNA to produce non-failing, innovative technological design and to manufacture solutions to whatever new challenge a racing day produces the need for – and do it fast.

These teams have a core business of racing fast cars, but the very skills that enable the cars to race fast and safely are transferable. These have been applied in collaboration with the medical professions and others as urgent challenges demanded help.

Specific work streams in Project Pitlane faced a clearly defined challenge. One of the first involved collaboration between Mercedes-AMG Petronas Formula One Team, University College London (UCL), and UCL Hospitals NHS Foundation Trust (NHS is the UK's National Health Service).

*This is a great illustration*
*of what can be achieved by collaboration*
*– and it is an inspiration.*

**The urgent need**: a respiratory device Italy to help breathing when oxygen is not succeeding alone. It had to be produced rapidly in volumes of thousands on a design based on that used successfully in China.

**Result:** Starting on Wednesday 18th March, this work stream began.
- Within 100 hours a prototype was developed.
- The resulting device was approved for use by the British Medicines and Healthcare Products Regulatory Agency (MHRA).
- The products were manufactured and delivered to NHS hospitals in the first weeks of May, less than eight weeks later.

This speed of assessment, reengineering, prototype production, regulatory approval, manufacture, and delivery to needed sites, is why I say this is not normal – new or otherwise.

Re-deploying talent and their supporting resources has never had a more vivid poster boy than F1. This is an environment where each of the individual teams is fiercely competitive and secretive about their R&D. Yet the need surpassed individual grandstanding or team protection of knowledge and skills.

On 26th May 2020, on a global broadcast of 'The Competitiveness Institute', a global economic development association in which I have held membership for over 20 years (and in its early days was on its Board for the Americas), we heard of similar responses from Upper Austria and Denmark. As our focus in the association is the development of industry clusters, the broadcast focused on the benefit of already having developed these trust relationships between cluster members. This existing trust relationship shortened response time in developing needed solutions within various clusters and within the companies of their members.

Relationships forged through urgency of need and common sense of vital purpose, sustain – and who knows what they will develop in the future.

### *During Covid:*
Inditext *(the clothing label ZARA)* and local textile start-ups pivoted lines to manufacture PPE during Covid. This strengthened the supply chain and partnerships.

***Post Covid*:**
The company now invests more in regional and circular fashion systems – and that may prove a substantial advantage in current times.

***During Covid:***
Uber offered transport for vaccines, patients, and healthcare workers in Europe.

***Post Covid:***
This led to a dedicated arm of business in partnership with insurers. Now, a new branch of business 'Uber Health' provides non-emergency medical transport.

In developing your collaboration be aware of cultural and regional differences.

In the 'The Borderless World'[23], Kenichi Ohmae stresses the need for flexibility in whatever partnership or collaborative relationship you work.

Especially where there is a cultural difference of geography or language, don't expect responses to mirror yours. Find out the real basis for a response you didn't expect. Try to visualise what the other party's interpretation may be, or what the problems might be from the other end, but don't take your interpretation as the reality – ASK.

I worked with a company developing and supplying component products to customer specification. If there was

---

[23] The Borderless World', Kenichi Ohmae

any variance in expected communication from manufacturer or a customer, the principal of this company had a dangerous habit of making assumptions about why. Most of these proved totally false. But the time it took to realign wandering direction following actions based on these false assumptions, plus the time spent soothing ruffled feathers caused by un-empathetic communication could have been better invested in other more positive aspects of the business growth.

It is easier to get to the cause if you have already taken the time to develop personal relationships and friendships. If you haven't and it's a new relationship, even at a distance you can 'bond' through some non-mainstream personal connection time with your counterpart in another company - and possibly even between both families.

Growth through collaboration can hasten and refine the speed to your common objectives. In 'Antifragile[24]' by Nassim Nicholas Taleb there is a pertinent quotation:

*Wind extinguishes a candle and energizes a fire.*
*Likewise with randomness, uncertainty, chaos:*
*you want to use them, not hide from them.*

Taleb goes on to point out that volatility comes from the Latin *'volare'* - to fly, and that to be 'antifragile' means not merely to be robust or resilient. The resilient and robust withstand shocks and remain the same whereas the *antifragile* is altered and made stronger by the shock.

---

[24] Antifragile, Nassim Nicholas Taleb - My version printed in 2010

You want to be antifragile. As Taleb explains, this will enable you to:...be able to deal with the unknown, do things without understanding them and do them well.

Taleb also points out that we are much better at doing than thinking, so we need to get started.

*This is not a time for long-term planning.*
*Be expedient, creative, and courageous.*

## Don't start with cutting staff

I urge you not to make your immediate reaction one to downsize unless you have a clear cut case. We caution about the frequently applied knee-jerk, accountant-led approach that: 'staff are your highest cost – therefore: cut staff'.

Staff cuts may seem to be the obvious solution to improve a bottom line – but this is short-term thinking if it is your first response.

Firing or laying-off your people is the type of thinking that may well ditch the business in the future for lack of the same talent that departed, talent that may well give companies that *Swivel* a solid and sustainable advantage.

If there are obvious challenges for that path to be successfully negotiated and these mean needed staff may be fewer, then it is up to the whole team to identify and help initiate new ventures or employment opportunities with those not suited to that terrain.

Instead, to quote from Tom Peters in 'Thriving on Chaos':

*Turn everyone into a vacuum-cleaner.*

Get them examining your products like forensic scientists. Examine the "So What?" of everything. Break into small teams and attack each one of your products or value propositions as an experiment that needs modification to be adept for current times and future chaotic impacts.

As you are in this together with your supply chain and fulfillment teams, your ability to successfully map this new terrain effectively is better together than alone. To illustrate, let's review another case from Italy.

In the beautiful valley between Padua and Venice, over 500 small and medium sized businesses contribute to the output of the globally respected shoe-making industry that nestles along the Riviera del Brenta[25].

While attending an OECD workshop on industry clusters, some of us were fortunate enough to travel from Venice to see this remarkable collaboration first hand.

Along this valley almost all branded footwear of the world is produced – most often in co-design with the shoemakers of this region. But when faced with the economic crash of the 1990s, some firms couldn't survive

---

[25] https://artsandculture.google.com/exhibit/footwear-of-riviera-del-brenta/AR-6ec8-

and had to close – meaning a potential loss of skilled craftspeople. However, their 'Collective' maintains a central database of skills and it actively sought out new employment in other companies in the valley to take on the displaced staff.

There are over 10,000 highly skilled artisans in the shoe making business in the valley. The companies there realise that if these skills are lost to the region it is more than unemployment – it is the future diminishment of a critical skill base. During the impacts of the 1990s downturn, all who departed one company closing in the valley found jobs within in the local industry.

In response to the changed marketplace caused by the economic crisis, they made a collective *Swivel*.

On that Zoom broadcast with 'The Competitiveness Institute' we discussed previously, we heard how clusters in Denmark – which, in a key study ranked as the 8th most innovative of countries – were funding their own innovative businesses that were struggling. Like the Italian leatherworkers, they recognise that to lose a key component of the value chain diminishes the whole.

But back to our Italian shoemakers.

The economic crash of the 1990s severely damaged the shoemakers' traditional markets. This led them to *Assess* their collective core value. They then matched that to the best market where the benefits that core offered would be appropriately appreciated and rewarded.

# SWIVEL

The shoemakers agreed that their core skill was superb quality and craftsmanship. Therefore, they needed to **Refocus** on the high-end markets where quality and craftsmanship are paramount and valued – and to take their products to the fashion capitals not as a group of shoemakers, but in collaboration as a regional brand with other relevant products serving that same high-value market. This was well-aided by the fact that their region – that of the broader Venice area - already had (and has) recognition from their chosen market segment.

Then it was time to **Act.** Our shoemaking cluster reached out to Venice with their focus on fine glassware and exquisite Venetian food. Together with the highly-valued leatherwork products of the Riviera del Brenta, these made an impressive showing of regional branding – adding value for all three collaborators.

This caused then to **Succeed**: Because that combination also added value to the chosen customer segment, the results were immediate and have sustained.

That is the power of an effective **Swivel**.

The Brenta Master Shoemaker Consortium logo reflects the rich history of craftsmanship on which current success is built. The seal of the Congregation of Shoemakers in Venice dates from 1268. In 1898 the Cobblers Confraternity moved under the same seal to the Riviera del Brenta and the ancient craft of shoemaking became an industry.

Impacted by the Financial Crisis of 2007-8, the shoemaking cluster's collective didn't wait for the torturous path of bureaucracy to grant them funds for a polytechnic. They started with the master shoemakers and their top-skilled teams and started their own, growing it from the roots of the former school of Footwear Design and Technology founded in 1923. Teachers taught on weekends after plying their trade during the week. Times have moved on, and now this self-developed Politecnico Calzaturiero (Footwear Polytechnic) draws students from around the world.

In his book 'The Mind of the Strategist', my version printed in 1982, Kenichi Ohmae gives a similar example: at that time, NEC had embraced manufacturing automation. Recognising its vulnerability from a growing dependence on government contracts, the company set out to grow service to the wider business community. This meant a strategic change of focus. What could have been massive layoffs were avoided by those staff being retrained into computer programming or external sales. Despite the massive reduction of needed production staff, through redeployment NEC also laid off no one.

In ' Managing in Turbulent Times', Peter Drucker recommends that redundancy planning should be a process involving staff and unions because it offers opportunities.

By contrast, an example I used in my book Shrapnel Free Explosive Growth, was that of an airline whose account-led 'cut staff' mandate was effectively carried out according to union specifications of "last in – first" out.

Only one problem: The last aircraft type added to the fleet was BAC-111 and all of these were due critical checks.

Aircraft require A, C, and D checks: The *A Check* happens every 8-10 weeks. Filters are changed, key systems like hydraulics in control surfaces are lubricated, and all emergency equipment is inspected.

*C Checks* are needed every 18 months to two years (depending on utilisation and the type of aircraft) and are more extensive.

The *D Check* is essentially a complete dismantling of the whole aircraft – engines off – the lot – so that the skin of the aircraft can be inspected. It's a case of all landing gear taken off and overhauled and all systems and parts inspected, refurbished, or replaced according to strict guidance. This process takes 3 to 6 weeks.

As you can see – each of these requires workers trained, skilled, and certified on that particular type of aircraft – in the case of the BAC-111s, the same people who had just been let go.

The accountants hastily said "Hire them back!"

Reportedly, the universal reply was along the lines of "Pardon me? I am now working for XXXX Air – at a much higher salary. Why would I come back?"

In recent time of writing, in April 2025, similar 'slash and burn' layoffs of key staff who keep the wheels running has taken place across the USA. As Mark Cuban was quick to point out, these skilled people have a chance to set up their own companies to supply the services that are essential but now without government staffing.

Perhaps this is a niche that you could be filled by hiring some of that experience.

In the Inc Live streamed presentation interviewing Clay Smith who grew his company through the financial crash, his first point was never to lay off your staff if it can be avoided. At the signs of the market downturn, Smith cut his own salary plus R&D and product development and the people weathered the storm together.

Smith was honest with his people. He says that he had responsibilities to them and their families and they could work through it as a team. He believes that losing people is the one thing you cannot afford and that in his case it set the company in great standing for the ensuing 10 years. His overall message is the same as ours: *we are all in this together*.

*This he demonstrated by sharing the wealth with his staff when he later sold the company for $500 million.*

Inc editorial intern Gabrielle Bienasz has summarised the content – link below[26] and perhaps the video will still be there for you to watch. It was at the time of writing.

---

[26] https://www.inc.com/gabrielle-bienasz/big-ass-fans-carey-smith-recession.html?utm_source=incthismorning

It is a case study on thriving despite what happens, and doing so through honestly sharing the problems and the problem-solving with your own teams.

It is also a case study in seeing the positives of the situation and building from there, and of sharing the benefits of success, just as you together shared the difficulties.

These examples may prompt you to think before addressing staff issues. ...and besides which – if you don't yet have a future plan, how can you effectively staff it?  In the words of Father Thoedore Hesburgh, the former President of Notre Dame University in America:

*You can't blow an uncertain trumpet.*

It may even be that your competitors – or those you thought were your competitors – are part of your forward path: collaboration may make sense and collaborative staffing might be the corner piece of that collaboration jigsaw.

In my current firm, Archer Business Group Europe, we have worked with companies facing such dilemmas as the enormous overhead of staff costs in times of crisis – admittedly in not such a radically changed environment as that which we now face.

We always start by suggesting this 'whole team' approach. It is truly inspiring how much gold is lying unattended in the valleys you seldom visit within your own organisation. In our experience, some of that gold dust has suggested directions that later overtook what previously had been the main game.

In every instance, there have been productive results that came directly as a result of new perspectives from the valley floor. These caused a different level of review than would otherwise have happened without their input.

You've also got to "get a whiff" of what is happening in the future for your clients and your supply chain. The only way to do so is to get out there and have a short-sleeved 'Get a Whiff' meeting.

If you think collectively first, then act in response to objective review, but still find the need to part with some of your existing staff, if you have involved them, it should make the rift easier for both sides.

Parting with employees can take on a new and more productive approach as you work with them to make a better transition from your company to the next. This leaves your company reputation intact and offers genuine support for departing staff to not slink into the future, but fly. Realities are to be faced, and staff loss may be inevitable, but like all bad news, the impact is often mitigated by the way it is handled.

Build on your values.

Don't think that the world isn't watching how companies respond to external pressures from officialdom – and marking the cards of those who show disdain or disregard for what are believed to me previous ethics, and customer or staff loyalty.

In the current volatile political environment your customers are also noting the companies who "sell out" either to gain value for themselves by trying to make political capital, or by responding to demands which are contrary to their once clearly stated values.

These days, consumers are a canny lot. The price you pay for a cavalier attitude towards your employees, your customers, and your communities and their needs may be much larger and last much longer than you would think. Also, don't underrate the service jobs that surround you and how your company can impact them or serve them.

'The Big Reset[27]' was written by Richard Florida in response to the economic crisis of 2009-10 caused by anomalies of banking (to put it politely). In the book, Florida talks about the importance of service jobs. From his book it appears that where the workforce is made up of a high percentage of service jobs, there is a correlation with

*"higher levels of economic output, productivity, innovation, new business start-ups and significantly higher levels of happiness and well-being."*

There have been many posts and news articles along the same lines of this admonition by Florida that just patching up the past isn't good enough. He wrote:

*We must design a better future-*
*not just for our companies*
*but also for the wider community.*

If you approach this most critical time in the whole experience of your company – and of the world - with input from your own team and agree that '*We are all in this together*' you will have the richest resources to adjust your

---

[27] The Big Reset, Richard Florida – My version printed in 2010

future to the best options. We all know that such times of total re-creation of the former order always open new avenues previously unconsidered or undiscovered. These avenues may prove to build a better and more resilient organisation. They certainly can provide new inspiration to each member of your existing team.

*'Sometimes to be reborn, you first have to die'* is an old Chinese proverb.

We don't plan on your company dying, but you may have to shrink to grow. Don't be afraid of removing what doesn't add value to your organisation: rules, processes, products, methods, or technology. It may be that your products might need to die and be reborn as part of a service value chain that you lead. If this *is* the need, then with your teams work out what that could mean if you approached it creatively.

Even in this slimming down there is opportunity – to create small spin off companies, to form specific collaborations - there are lots of creative options beside the obvious one of shrinkage plain and simple. In 'The Long Tail'[28], Chris Anderson identified that the biggest market is in the smallest sales. He labels it a 'market of multitudes'. This has since been questioned, but it is worth exploring. Seek out the small niche markets.

The purpose of your collective **Swivel** is to gather the widest possible input.  Take input, but you will have to make the hard decisions yourself.  To manage expectations, make it clear from the outset that *input* does not equate to decision-making.

Good luck, and as you embark on this new journey, remember the words of Peter Drucker from 'Managing in

---

[28] The Long Tail, Chris Anderson - My version printed in 2006

Turbulent Times'[29], and written in the context of the 'new technologies' and emerging global markets. This was when the personal computer was making its debut and old patterns of business were visibly disrupting:

*The greatest danger in times of turbulence*
*is not the turbulence;*
*it is to act with yesterday's logic.*

With his usual prescience, Drucker continued to predict that the next challenge would be **structural change** rather than one of modification, extension, and/or exploitation. He could be writing of our times, for fiddling around the edges won't do – we all need a serious rethink and to make our own efforts to create the sort of structural change we believe can make our world a better place – and your business more successful.

In 'Hope is not a Method', the authors offer something else good to remember.

*Barnstormer's 1st rule of wing-walking:*
*Don't let go with both hands at once.*

We recognise that there are two challenges to the leader of change: that of managing the business so it doesn't fall over, and that of creating the right path towards the right products and services, with the right organisational underpinning, and the right staff, with the right empowerment to get the job done – and the right finances to do so. So – don't let go with both hands at once.

We expect that what this book is doing is allowing you to hold onto the existing structure as it hurtles over uncharted territory. It might be that as you hang on you

---

[29] Managing in Turbulent Time, Peter Drucker - My version printed in 1980

notice some rivets moving in alarming patterns in and out of the infrastructure, but it is holding together well enough.

From your high point of perspective you can see things more clearly to map a path forward – and never forget that the crowd on the ground is watching.

As your company emerges into this vastly changed – and rapidly changing world, we must assess the health of the business to see:

- what is working,
- what isn't working,
- what can be retrofitted, and
- what needs replacing or stripping off altogether-

and all this in terms of radically changed customer priorities, and also perhaps the changed capabilities of your supply chain and fulfillment partners.

In doing so, be honest and don't favour the things you personally like – this is about assessing your business suitability to the current needs of a vastly changed marketplace and even more vastly changed consumer. No matter what your favourite thing about your business offer is, it may no longer hold its relevance.  So let's go forward together and *Swivel* so we can Assess, Refocus, Act – and Succeed.

*Change the changeable. Accept the unchangeable
and remove yourself from the unacceptable.*

Denis Waitley

# CHAPTER TWO
# Where is here?

*The first priority of a leader is to define reality.*

Max de Pree – Leadership is an Art

'Leadership is an art[30]' is a book that is the baseline for the empowerment of employees in the entire global operation of furniture company Herman Miller. I know this from personal experience.

One of our clients used to annually ship pallet loads of donated goods to the island of Dominica where they were distributed by a charity there. Naturally, it was a case of all hands on deck when the shipment was being assembled for pick-up.

In later shipments, as a consultant to the company, apart from assembling packages onto pallets and emergency covering of the goods in the case of delays coinciding with heavy downpours, it fell to me as part of this pro bono work, to deal with the transport. Herman Miller consistently and cheerfully arranged for one of their trucks to carry the load to Southampton Docks from a small town near Bath, in England. Unfailingly, the drivers were exceptionally helpful. The manager was a delight to deal with – and this quiet polishing of brand has had a lot of appreciation and notice.

---

[30] Leadership is an Art, Max de Pree - My version printed in Australia in 1989

I recommend the book. It hasn't sold over 800,000 copies for nothing.

## ASSESS

The whole assessment process is one of reviewing and qualifying what you all thought to be facts. As Robert H. Thouless pointed out in 'Straight and Crooked Thinking[31]' settling a question of fact can *only* be done by observation or research – so with that in mind, let's proceed and do both.

### *Accurate positioning*

In the book 'Leadership is an Art', de Pree tells the story of driving near Southampton, in England, and having a discussion with his wife about whether the water alongside which they were driving was the English Channel or the Falmouth estuary, where the Spanish Armada saw its demise.

They pulled to the side of the road and asked a pedestrian if this was the English Channel. The dry English response from the pedestrian, after looking over his shoulder towards the body of water in question, was: "It's part of it".

You need to be more specific than that in defining where you are.

To assess effectively so that you can plan forward, you need a baseline that shows where you are starting - and you

---

[31] Straight and Crooked Thinking, Robert H. Thouless - My version printed in 1958

need this health check fast. So, I have started on some lists that may prove helpful as you do so.

These lists are not definitive – they are a prompt.
Expand.
Delete.
Add.
Make them your own.

This is just a way to organise your thinking when the myriad responsibilities you face are overtaxing your brain. Together with your team assess the current state of:

## THINGS
- Equipment.
- Facilities.
- Fleet.

## OPERATIONS
- Regulatory compliance, certifications and licences.
- Health and probability of remaining in business of your supply-chain and fulfillment partners
- Security of wider supporting business relationships.
- Finance and availability of cash reserves and investment. If your market has suddenly shut down as unprofitable. How long can you sustain? This will give you an urgency framework within which to work.
- Warehousing and inventory: It is essential that you have accurate and current real-time numbers to evaluate so you can estimate the impact of tariffs and cessation of supply lines (At time of writing several countries postal systems and international freight carriers are not accepting packages to the

USA as they are not in a position to collect the taxes as required by new regulations.)
- Status and possible future of 'in flight' projects (those that were underway and should be closed down or put on hold until future plans are more concrete).
- Effectiveness of current physical staff office and home working arrangements.

## PEOPLE
- Staff morale. (We may be aware that we need to broadcast 'out there' about our business, but more urgently you need to broadcast 'in there', something we will deal with later in the book).
- Supply chains, professional services and fulfillment partners. (This is different than that above. This is not an operational check of their businesses. It is a check on the relationships developed between your teams and theirs and perhaps between their leaders and you. There may be something that you glean from this checking-in that helps both organisations to survive. At the very least, it is in line with your values, or should be.

## MARKET
- Relevance of your products and/or services.
- Immediately identifiable risks and opportunities.
- Identified 'Wobble-Points' and 'Building Blocks'.

**Wobble points** emerge where activities have not generated expected results. Perhaps your technology was not up to the sudden thrust of usage hitherto unpredicted and therefore not provided for – or being able to discriminate effectively between a client's (or individual's) *critical needs* or their *urgent needs*.

It may be that you redeployed staff for activities that were essential – or for which you were well equipped to respond in times of crisis  but that generate no tangible profit – wildfires, tornadoes, floods, and Covid come to mind. That may have caused a wobble point – but it may also have given you a building block for new business.

**Building blocks** are the aspects of your business or products or of the way you go about things that have been a surprise – a good surprise, because they highlighted a resilient capacity or an important benefit you had not understood to be resident within the company.

We will return to 'Wobble Points' and 'Building Block's later. For now, as you go through your assessment, just place a W or BB beside any relevant thing. This is part observation, part intuition.

Bear in mind your intuition may not be based on sufficient evidence, so we are actually identifying where we need to do more questioning and more interpretation of the answers to those questions, to be sure we framed the question in its most useful manner.

So let's start systematically. Before we can assess effectively and draw a useful baseline, we need to clarify what that baseline means.

Is it: 'Fit for business for the future' or 'Fit for the business as it is'. It can be either – or even both – that is up to you, but you should be clear about exactly what your baseline is setting out to measure and not expect it to give information other than that. Getting the parameters straight before you begin is worth the effort involved, because you don't have time to do this twice. In the words of Abraham Lincoln:

*Give me six hours to chop down a tree*
*and I will spend the first four sharpening the axe.*

So sharpen your axe by answering a most important question.

### What is your core business?

Most people think this is easy to answer and maybe it once was, but even before you were encompassed by massive changes in the world order that are affecting the market of everyone, your definition was probably inadequate.

How can I be so sure? Experience.

Let's expand on that by examining value in each of the following examples. I will highlight an obvious core business value – but as we will see, the actual value as perceived by the customer may vary considerably from that perceived by you. In italics I will add an alternative value/core.

**Perhaps you are in the non-commercial real estate business** and think you represent both buyers and sellers. Is that your core business? Or is it that you are a matchmaker between people seeking a new home and those with homes for sale, **reducing the stress at both ends of the house sale transaction**.

**OR** Developing trust with house buyers and sellers so that your facilitation will shorten the cycle, minimise the paperwork, and arrive at a fair price for both parties.

**If you have a technology company**, perhaps you believe your core business is using technology to solve problems. The nature of the problems you solve might vary dramatically from the way it is perceived by those applying it to national security, policing, or emergency services – or e-commerce. Your core business here may be, in each case respectively thought to be **solving refinements in data interpretation – or ease of buying and selling online.**

**OR** 'Becoming a valuable extension of the customers current business that helps ... (respectively) accurate information getting to the right people with the right detail at the right time so they can make the right critical decisions' - or 'giving information about a product in such a way that it speeds the online sales transaction and minimises returns, while maintaining accurate inventory and predicting trends'.

**Perhaps you operate a fleet of vehicles or ships or aircraft**. Maximising revenue from the best organisation of the end-to-end operation of the transport network could be considered your core business.

**OR** (assuming these to be cargo carrying)being an extension of the client shipper and their receiver, to make sure that we get loads to the right place, at the right time, and with no damage, with  minimal investment of time in handling paperwork, yet being completely verifiable.

**OR** (assuming you are in the leisure transportation and holiday business) Becoming the host of choice for people wanting to have a vacation that minimises decision making, gives the right options for the market segment, and creates an end-to-end pleasurable experience.

To help you isolate what is your current core business so that you understand implications better, ask yourself **what value is delivered to your customer from the functionality of your business or service** – and then ask *why* that is valuable.

Here is a classic example, if somewhat light hearted example of a core value proposition. It nonetheless demonstrates how to manifest intangible value into some sort of reality to the consumer.

I confess to having long been a Chanel girl. Like others who are attracted to a product, it reflects how I like to think of myself – rightly or wrongly – but only recently did I start to purchase directly online from Chanel. Wow!

My parcel arrived in a smart unlabelled white box. I guess one wouldn't want to create what in insurance terms is called 'an attractive nuisance' by tempting light fingers with that smart black brand name on the outside. There is an easy-open rip-strip and when I open the box; 'CHANEL' is imprinted on the underside of the open outside lid. Inside sits an elegant black- edged high quality box with the brand marked on the top in raised, shiny black letters.

The inside of the box is black and my purchased products are separated by concertina folds of white tissue, and found after releasing a black shiny Chanel seal. The lot sits on shredded white tissue.

My tempter 'gifts' (I know I pay for all them – *and* the packaging – in the price) sit within fine quality, black drawstring bags of what is probably silk rayon. I could describe with equal admiration other little boxes and packages that have arrived from Chanel, similarly detailed. Each has a stylish card within, hoping I will enjoy the products and telling me the first name of the person who packed them.

Does this sit with my expectations of a brand that has stood for simplicity, style and elegance since Coco opened her first shop in Paris in 1910? Oh yes.

Is it worth it to me to buy Chanel? Oh yes.

In 2004, when Nicole Kidman was wooed to represent Chanel No. 5 in a 2 minute mini-film after her Academy Award Nomination role in *Moulin Rouge!* , Vogue magazine[32] interviewed Chanel president, Françoise Montenay to ask "Why Nicole, and why spend this much money on the campaign?"

*At that time Chanel No. 5*
*was reportedly generating between $10 and $12 million in*
*annual sales.*

---

[32] https://www.vogue.co.uk/article/the-chanel-icon

We may have our views of what business Chanel is in – but we may be very wrong.

*Chanel knows what business it is in:*
*not couture,*
*not perfume,*
*not cosmetics, or skin care.*

Mme. Montenay responded that just as Chanel No. 5 was an icon – so was Nicole (I would add – 'and always a lady' – an image Chanel fosters) – and went on to say (**Bold** *is mine*):
*What we are very good at*
*is to work with the imagination of women.*
***We make them dream.***

Isolate your core business as succinctly. It may well be quite different from what you thought it was.

I recount in 'Shrapnel Free Explosive Growth' how, when I worked with an airline they first decided that they their core offer was in selling aircraft seats. After we did a collective ***Swivel*** this changed to a two-fold business core:

- Making business travel a seamless and enjoyable experience that removes stress.
- Delivering the dream of a carefree holiday in exotic destinations, with no complications in getting there and back.

This fundamentally changed the whole business model, marketing focus, and customer relationship efforts. That 'Why?' should be from the customer's perspective, not yours. We will go into this a bit more later.

Once you have that answer it will be important to ruminate on whether that is still the need of the same customers – or have their needs segmented, changed priority, or altered in any other way? Or do you see a whole new customer family better suited to what you have to offer?

Your answer doesn't have to be perfect. It should be thoughtful and expedient. You can change this definition because you are doing a diagnostic and that always lays out the terrain between where you are and where you need to be.

Our Dad always taught us – ***all good reconnaissance is 90% negative information.*** So what if your answer isn't exact right now? Give one. It's a yardstick. It is a yardstick for assessment of current business health.

### Take stock of where you are vs. the future
This 'taking stock' is a huge task. It is a critical task– and it cannot wait. Therefore, as you identify the health of each component of your organisation, assign it a quality. This way you can group things that have some associative elements.

In 'Patterns in the Sand: Computers, Complexity, and Life'[33], , the authors, Terry Bossomaier and David Green, talk about dealing with complexity by using examples from

---

[33] Patterns in the Sand: Computers, Complexity, and Life, Terry Bossomaier and David Green - My version published in Australia in 1998

nature and science. They write that complexity comes from the way things are put together.

*We move from the merely complicated –*
*lots of elements - to the complex –*
*the interrelationship of those elements.*

They point out that to understand, it is not enough to disassemble the complex. You have to be able to put things back together again in more meaningful ways.

The good news is that it is often from this examination and disassembly and the examination of simple principles something emerges that has unexpected wide application.

So, with this admonition of Ernest Bramah in mind let's go forward:

*Where the road ends abruptly, take short steps.*

Here is a table that may be useful as you **Swivel.** So you can start out with small steps, using something like this is one way to group things so you can know what needs immediate attention, and these include:

- What to save, but that might need to be reviewed for effectiveness in this fast pace of global change.
- Where you could 'whittle'(reduce), invest, evolve, or leverage to another purpose beyond the original.

Let's use **_Swivel_** as an acronym (with apologies for making 'Leverage' into a verb):

**S**ave

**W**hittle

**I**nvest

**V**erify

**E**volve

**L**everage

The column **VERIFY** needs your attention. It needs your attention in putting the right things in it – and it needs your attention in being honest with yourself and your team about what reality tells you. Reality may differ from what you expect(ed).

It may differ because these are elements to which you have an emotional attachment – you developed them – or they were the original key or core things, etc.

It may differ because you are now asking for all those charts to be translated into meaning. In 'The Average is Always Wrong', Ian Shepherd warns us that a 20% average is disguising interesting nuances.

Why is it made up of such variance?

Why is one group only at 2%?

Get underneath and find out what your data is trying to tell you. A neat chart is not giving you the information you need. Perhaps your data shows a best-selling product. In another set of silo data it may reveal that this best-selling product is generating most of the Help Desk calls due to some malfunction or lack of clarity in its supporting documentation.

It may differ because you relied upon individuals and not a system and the individuals are no longer in place to take those actions and something went (or is going) wrong. This is usually due to what I call the *'Trust your mother but cut the cards'* method not being in place.

Your systems should not rely on individual integrity or you can put someone at risk for unwittingly compromising the outcome. A system should eliminate – or at least reduce the chance of – accidental errors. If you have a system, you can trace the crumbs back to Hansel and Gretel's house before you get eaten by the big bad wolf – to mix fairy tales.

Having identified that the birds are eating your crumbs, you either strip previous activities out, design better ones, or patch - so the crumb-eating birds don't think you have provided them with a free smorgasbord.

As Edward de Bono points out in 'The Textbook of Wisdom'[34], your perception is telling you (the collective 'you') more than what you see with your eyes. It is what your individual and collective brains do with that information that makes it 'perceptive'.

In that context, your perception may differ because your team tells you one thing but your intuition tells you

---

[34] The Textbook of Wisdom', Edward de Bono - My copy printed in 1996,

something else. In this case do the verification but trust your gut.

In 'Blink[35]: The Power of Thinking Without Thinking', Malcolm Gladwell encourages us to listen to that intuition because it is based on an accumulation of background information. As he says, we need to accept that sometimes we know without knowing why we know.  This is borne out by research documented by Gerd Gigerenzer in 'The Intelligence of Intuition '[36]where his definition is that intuition is a feeling:

- Based on long experience
- That appears quickly into one's consciousness, and
- Whose underlying rationale is unconscious.

You and your teams have long experience with your organisation. Your intuition will help make sense of what you find when you *Swivel*.

Expand the table or build one of your own.  This one is just a prompt. We all need a starting point. It is like reading a draft of an important letter. It is quicker to write something when it has been started in draft.  You are more effective at editing something begun, than beginning with a blank sheet of paper.

I trust that the grid on the following page helps organise your thinking – even if it just prompts you to

---

[35] Blink: The Power of Thinking Without Thinking, Malcolm Gladwell – My copy printed in 2005
[36] The Intelligence of Intuition, Gerd Gigerenzer – My copy printed in 2023

make a better one.  The objective is to assign things into logical groups based on the observations of your initial group Swivel.  Once so listed you can qualify each for the validity of where it sits and this in turn gives you another Swivel opportunity to refine your judgement and isolate the essence of what must be the immediate task at hand.

When you are evaluating your assessment of the organisation and start asking questions about that current state and the opportunities and needs of the future, if the answers don't seem logical –Daniel Kakneman suggest in 'Thinking Fast and Slow[37]' that you reframe the question. Reframing the question very often changes the answer to something more succinct, realistic and/or meaningful.

In 'New Think'[38], author Edward de Bono uses a series of exercise to show how we can reframe our perspective and therefore our thinking.  De Bono first makes the point that in trying to define the problem we tend to use familiar expressions that echo traditional thinking. He suggests things like not describing a house as having walls that hold up the roof but a roof that has walls suspended from it. (Don't go with total accuracy but with a creative alternative description).

In the book, De Bono reminds us of the folly of describing things in ways that are based on the (possibly flawed) thinking that created the problem in the first place. He reminds us that when we *break down a physical thing*

---

[37] Thinking Fast and Slow, Daniel Kakneman - My version printed in 2012

[38] New Think, Edward de Bono – My version printed in 1968

into its component parts to examine each component for its own possibilities and limitations, we can put it back together again, so it doesn't matter in what way we disassemble it ('damage avoidance' being the watchword). The benefit of arranging the pieces in fanciful and unlikely relationships to each other and to other things – and in laying them out haphazardly in harmonious relationships can create some answers that are unexpected.

Sometimes that physical breakdown – even if only done verbally or in sketches, can lead to quite new ways of describing the problem. However, the process of breaking *an explanation* into component parts has different qualities. De Bono reminds us these 'explanation pieces' do not have an existence as such, and so once broken down, the aggregated reassembly is not necessarily a valid representation of the whole.

I was happy that the book also endorses the sorts of analogies that are employed throughout this book – like those you will meet on future pages: the Gin Gate and the creatures that live in your IT applications portfolio.

De Bono is an advocate of 'playing' with the problem.

The very peculiarities of the playthings you create or the fun ways that you label something can force an extension of that humour to what at first seems ridiculous - but that very often reveals the critical element of a solution.

As de Bono says:

*The play process can turn up **interesting patterns***
*that become added to the repertoire of familiar figures*
*and are just as useful as those acquired*
*during description of unfamiliar figures.*

In 'The Textbook of Wisdom', de Bono reminds us that there are always 'possibilities' – and these are the opposite of certainty. He also wrote that when the cause of progress isn't an accident, it comes from the generation and exploration of those possibilities. In 'New Think' he makes another important point:

*Problems are the jolts that shift things*
*out of the smooth rut of mere **adequacy.***

Bear in mind as you ***Swivel*** that *adequate* is not good enough.

Put each element of your assessment in the appropriate box of the table below.

| Save | Whittle | Invest-igate | Verify | Evolve | Leverage |
|------|---------|--------------|--------|--------|----------|
| *S* | *W* | *I* | *V* | *E* | *L* |
| Every fit for purpose element goes here – all the things that were proven under stress of the un-expected. | How simple can you make it? | Enter here the things that don't seem to fit any more; things that don't make sense for the world of now; things that spark your interest -things that make you ask 'Why?' | These are the things you had better get right or risk some penalty. What does your market think of your offer? (good & bad – and how do you know?) | These are the way you did things before the world tilted on its axis where you can tinker to improve so you respond best to changes as they arrive. | Here, go all the strength that emerged over Covid or during any other crisis that you faced– the things that are helping keep the boat afloat as global change creates waves. |

When completed it may look something like this:

| Save S | Whittle W | Investigate I | Verify V | Evolve E | Leverage L |
|---|---|---|---|---|---|
| Levels of staff empower -ment | Some expenses *W* Approvals process *W* | Facilities design | Licences | Fleet | Rel'ships with Supply Chain & partners *BB* |
| Comms channels | Equip't no longer suitable | Building - location and layout | Regs– re- assess | External supply chain | Profl network *BB* |

In the course of your assessment you may wish to consider some things we have learned from experience with our client companies - things that might otherwise be overlooked. I have put them below the relevant headings.

I have not here addressed legal or personnel issues because those fall into a category not the main focus of this book – which is rapid and detailed assessment of the current state of your business,; how it is currently impacted and may be further impacted, and how to design a resilient and robust forward plan so that you are, in Taleb's terms 'antifragile' as each new egg hatches from the Black Swan's nest.

The things not addressed, but which may still need to be done, include: the necessity to review business-continuity insurance to see if terms provide an opportunity to get financial assistance; review of standard contracts to see whether in the instance of being unable to deliver to commitment there are any applicable clauses;  how GDPR applies in the case of demands from government that are not in line with accepted legal practice; any legal contracts with unions or other representative bodies on how supply-chain induced slowdowns are to be handled.

But as we set out in our assessment, bear in mind this encouragement by IBM in the announcement of their second iteration of a Covid-19 Action Guide for Executives[39] (you can download it via the link in the footnote):

*When so much is still unknown, there is no one "right way"—only a mix of ever-evolving possibilities, and our conviction to create a better future. The goal is to propel those possibilities toward a vision of tomorrow. This crisis will pass. What comes next is up to us.*

So let's start the detailed assessment of the following. Add, delete, change, as makes the list sensible for your operations.

## THINGS
### *Divestment of 'things'*
You may identify what looks like insurmountable cost in 'things' – equipment, packaging types – all sorts of things whose current cost makes using them in the future seem prohibitive.

Don't make decisions on these until you consider all the options: leasing, resource-sharing with suppliers or even with customers – there are other options, explore them all.

We helped local governments in a rural Australian region group all their heavy equipment into one 'umbrella'

---

39 https://www.ibm.com/downloads/cas/BMWXZBRX

lease contract that moved expenses immediately from Capital to Operational cost and removed maintenance costs totally.

### Transportation of 'things'

One company in Australia was shipping fragile products by air and needed to cut the escalating packaging costs. They formed an alliance with a company shipping wool blankets, duvets (known as 'comforters' to the American readers), and pillows. Innovative packaging defrayed the cost to each company and resulted in damage free arrivals of the fragile items. If your equipment volumes are too small to attract a lease, think with whom you can bundle equipment to make it up to the necessary volume – even competitors may be good partners in this aggregation.

### Asset Inventory – what 'things' are immediately available

It is worth doing a rapid inventory of all your assets. 'Things' move.

Make it easy for staff to tell you where the 'things' that you cannot locate now reside without ANY implication of punitive responses for having done so – or it might remain a secret forever.

People may have done what was necessary and what was expedient under the circumstances – and these things probably seemed logical at the time.

Whatever was moved may have found a happy home in which to reside and the people who were the moving company that got it there may have left and somehow not mentioned the details to anyone.

Instances will be few where someone took advantage of the moment. It may be that it is an accident of fate with no mal-intent. Take that view and proceed accordingly with an expectation of honesty.

Where things are missing, make it public to your whole team – but not like school days where this was framed in the obvious outcome of shaming the culprit. An objective statement of what is missing and details of last known whereabouts will be sufficient. If this is communicated in the context of thanking everyone for the accounting of what has been moved elsewhere, then peer pressure might help resolve issues.

If you cannot find something, consider its real value before you respond.

You are in the business of restructuring. Unless it is absolutely a critical component – or a dangerous one in the wrong hands – write it off and get on with the main job of assessment and planning for a more adaptable and responsive future organisation.

### Suitability of 'things' to new needs
In the course of your assessment of 'things', note what appears to now be no longer fit for its original purpose. You don't need detail at this stage but jot down the 'what' and 'why' and make a note of the basis on which you make the judgement.

This allows for qualifying that judgement at a later date, for finding new uses, and defining the perceived incapacity in terms that makes replacement or alternatives easier to specify accurately.

## Information Technology needs

In recognition of the individuality of choice of home computers, some companies recognised that people may wish to use their own equipment.

If this preference was notable in the case of your company, ask yourself why. In many cases we have found that office computing equipment is considered old hat by people who demand much more capacity from their own home computers than that which is provided by the company. They therefore prove dismissive about an expectation to get sophisticated tasks done with such equipment, when their own would be preferable.

In frustration, many people just use their own equipment and this means that data that should be within your electronic security compound isn't.

It may be a time to discuss this dichotomy in terms of reality. You may be surprised by the wisdom, creativity and clarity of solutions offered by your own staff in meeting this challenge of differing expectations.

## EXTERNALS AND INTERNALS
### *Drivers of London Black Cabs and your organisation*

You need to find the Black Cab drivers in your organisation as you assess.

I choose the example of London's Black Cabs because of the uniqueness of their common talent and discipline. Each driver has already undergone incredible self-education to pass *'The Knowledge'*. This rigorous individual learning effort usually takes between two and four years of physically travelling the streets and back lanes of London until they and their interconnections are imprinted in the mind.

Candidates must be able to recall on demand specific directions from over 320 routes, 25,000 streets and around 20,000 landmarks within a six-mile radius of Charing Cross.

Before they can be issued with a licence to drive a black cab, potential drivers must demonstrate the ability to visualise routes from here to there (literally from any point in London to any other point) and first gain at least a 60% pass level on two written tests and then verbalise the answers on demand to examiners in three separate tests of increasing levels of difficulty.

*(Momentary pause to think about starting at Foyles Book Store to travel to Horse Guards in peak hour: 'Make a U turn, travel to the second intersection on the right into Shaftesbury Avenue, (to avoid Piccadilly Circus) take the third on the right into Wardour Street. Cross Orange Street to Haymarket. Turn right onto Pall Mall and right into Whitehall past the Earl Hague memorial, make a U turn and return to Horse Guards – entrance is on the left.)*

Such workforce discipline can therefore be expected to keep to a new stringent control for your safety, just as they adhere to others which make a black cab the vehicle of choice for any discerning traveller to London.

It is worth you identifying the 'Black Cab Drivers' in your own organisation.

These are the people who can close their eyes and visualise and recount precisely and unambiguously how a product/process works without having to consult any documents – and if you are redesigning, can alert you immediately to the exact reason why NOT to do something.

*'Black Cab Drivers' in organisations are usually highly under-rated and under-valued.*

Find them and consider how their knowledge can add further value to your company – and 'bottle it' *(find ways to package and either use it internally or sell it externally – or both).*

### Supply Chain Management

When considering your supply chain and your fulfillment partners, you may wish to do a little similar depth of research into what qualities and hiring parameters are used by the firms with whom you form associations and dependencies. They should match yours in ethos and expectation of discipline in responding to a level of standard performance.

It may make even more sense in the current global climate to work with your supply chain to have an integrated crisis response plan agreed.

In an article by Editor John Garratt in ITEuropa[40], 29th May 2020, the difference between the abilities of Dell and competitor HPE's ability to navigate the pandemic was largely due to the problems HPE had with "supply chain problems and order backlog deployments".

When I look at the link in the footer below I do wonder if they meant the word 'sails' or meant it to be 'sales'. Don't confuse *your* market with such ambiguity. Clarity aids uptake. If you wonder about the level of impact effective supply chain management can have, according to this article, despite the pandemic, Dell showed increased Year on Year profit for the period - by contrast, HPE registered loss. Dell is a master at relationships.

### *Suitability of the home office for hybrid or remote workers*

Not all home working spaces are created equal. Some of your teams have the luxury of a dedicated home office which they use for their own interests and hobbies. Others are limited to the kitchen table and have the interruptions of pets and children and spouses also working from home, sometimes at the other end of the same table.

Home work space might not be created equal, but all must be equal in terms of providing safe and ergonomically sound work environments. Provision of the right equipment and its servicing is your responsibility – not that of your team.

---

[40] https://www.iteuropa.com/news/dell-sails-profitability-despite-pandemic

Working out the 'how' of creating the most supportive home work spaces is going to require an individual approach and collaboration between your supervisory staff and their teams. Approach it in that vein – not in the manner of employing School Master discipline and inflexible (and unenforceable) rules.

## *Regulatory compliance, certifications and licences*
### Licences

Check the terms of key licence agreements. Expedience may have caused you to exceed your current licence agreements by adding more users, or by varying the operating platform from that which is designated, and where other platforms void your support agreement.

### Regulatory Environment

This is something we always suggest is scheduled to be checked regularly in what used to be considered normal times, let alone in a world where the evolution of regulations for the fast changing world is being influence by new data as it becomes available.

### *Maintenance*

From our experience it is worth really checking each relevant activity to ensure that maintenance was completed as per expectation. This will become even more important as shortages of some parts may be expected. There may be an inability to source some vital component, or someone may have been redeployed – or furloughed – in the midst of activities. Improvisation is fine – sometimes. Make sure that any is in line with all regulations and safety.

*Double check that what is thought to have been done, was actually done and done right.*

## Security of wider supporting business relationships

The time to discover impairments in your network of professionals who support your business is not when they are needed.

Make courteous 'health check' contact with external accountants, lawyers, landlords, insurers, those who handle you shipping documents and expedite your customs handling, the educational institutes where you source your new talent input and find out their status and how their plans impact yours. If they are no longer in a position to support you, finding new professionals who can needs to be one of your priority future actions.

### PEOPLE

In 'Thinking Fast and Slow', author Daniel Kakneman makes a useful point for us to add to our considerations about who is best suited to the roles of the company as it tackles a fast changing world. He points out that expertise is not a single skill but a collection of them and someone well-skilled in one domain may not excel in another.

I would add that the converse is also true and you may not have sufficient information about a person whose skills you are evaluating for a particular role if you only include in that evaluation the performance in his or her current domain. Dig deeper.

This is echoed by David Weinberg in 'Everything is Miscellaneous' when he points out that genius is topical - Einstein wasn't an expert in everything.

### *Staffing arrangements*

Value may not sit in the places you expect on your old organisational chart.

You may find the real value sits way lower down where your staff understand the product or service intimately and know the users and supply chain contacts as people, not as a company representative. This is your most valuable underground telegraph to alert you to trends – with negative positive potential impacts on your business - and it has point of view of your business as it stands today that is unobstructed by anything but operability. This is the 'whiff factor".

So when you take a 'we *are all in this together*' approach and involve your staff in defining opportunities in the fast changing world, ensure that you involve people at all levels.

How you do that is up to you. The most compelling results have come from those leaders who got out and went to the shop floor - and to the customer's shop floor – to really understand in a personal way what the future might hold.

---

[41] Everything is Miscellaneous, David Weinberg – My version printed in 2008

### *Staff re-deployment*

Do you know the key 'connectors' in all the organisations that are in your support or supply networks – and in your own company?  These are the people whose presence shortens communication and gives 'stickiness' to adherence to plans because of the relationships they have developed. If so, check that they haven't been removed from the place where they can achieve the most through this network they have built.

If not, then ask around the organisation – someone will know who these people are. Make a list of them and their networks. They are a valuable part of your new value proposition. These people fall into the same valuable category as your internal 'Black Cab Drivers'. In a similar way, identify people with key knowledge.

In the past, as the Chief Operations Officer for a software provider, our company had teams on client sites in six European countries and in South Africa. More often than one would have thought possible, our teams alerted us that the one key person for effectiveness of the operation they were supporting had been made redundant by the client company because their value had never been recognised – even when protests from within the organisation were made.

This was usually because the person heading the business unit thought things ran the way they once had – but that original process had long since mutated to more efficient pathways of working. Titles of those affected often seemed lowly and did not describe actual responsibilities, so they were literally struck off as expendable

It was the classic case of '*Don't confuse me with facts, my mind is made up*'.

They were let go. We immediately hired them.

Don't risk doing the same as those companies did.

Don't ask the business unit manager things about how real-time operations are structured today, without in some way including the people at the site face who can correct falsely based assumptions about how things work.

If you have business software that tracks your business processes, you may be able to see graphically how the 'should be' process has deviated from in the 'as is' process. The free software download of Aris by Software AG during Covid is just such a tool - and no – I receive no benefit from saying so. I am just a magpie collector of useful bits of information and in the past attended one of their information road-shows in London.

I generally dislike 'road-shows' as they usually proves self-serving rather than customer informative sessions – but the one I attended was cram packed with new, interesting , factual and applicable information that gives context to transformative change. As a result, I am now an extended part of their community because of the fact they add value – even to an outsider to their user group.

An example of how you can get wrong the way things work was demonstrated in a project where I worked with a major Scandinavian and Baltic bank.

In my assessments, I discovered that they had no idea that their Business Analysts needed computers and networks of the same quality and capacity as a Software Developer. This was due to the fact that a bank analyst needs to run business models on which major financial decisions are made – big, number-crunching models that needed the heft of an appropriate computer capacity. In the absence of the right equipment, staff improvised with equipment of their own – outside the security fences of usual requirements – and possibly inadvertently infringing regulatory compliance.

Working with a major energy supplier, I discovered that a gentleman with an insignificant title in terms of the organisational chart was the single potential point of failure in their financial decision-making. That was because he had developed a software program of his own to interrogate the Stock Exchange, and the output from these investigations was the basis on which all sales of their energy commodities were made. It was a system quite external to the main company systems – yet essential to their current business model. As I pointed out to them, if he was run over by a herd of fleeing camels they were in serious trouble.

The company asked how I knew. The answer was simple. I asked the individual what he did and how he used the company system. I asked because his role was not immediately obvious by title and influence.

In the same company they were surprised to find that the former shift pattern for their remote sites had changed.

It wasn't a major change, so wasn't thought worthy of being flagged to senior management – but when we were looking to make company-wide changes to the IT system, factoring in the correct shift pattern was essential so that the introduction to the new ways of working was not inadvertently missed by people on remote sites. You only discover such things when you get out and about to talk with people.

Without this check, it would have been assumed that an introduction to the changes would have taken place on a shift plan to which they were no longer assigned, or in groups that no longer existed, or had since fragmented.

Some of the parts of that fragmentation would have dropped into the ocean – or the desert – since these were people working on widely dispersed locations located in both environments. These sorts of 'oversight' issues are how accidents happen.

*People who should know, don't know*
*- because the people who do know don't make sure the*
*message gets through.*

So as you see, quite simple information can create a false baseline. Such things seem minor until we are in a situation where realistic and accurate evaluation is required – like in preparing for a radically changed and fast-changing business environment.

## Supply Chains and Fulfillment Partners

Do you know the pinch points in your supply chain and the critical 'single point of failure' of your component inventory? If you don't, the full implications of your current situation cannot be understood.

When are you renegotiating your contracts for shipments? For many these fall into annual phases, most of which were coming due for renewal at the time of writing with the May 5th 2025 deadline for changes to US imports. With no firm information in a period of volatile changes in tariffs, do you renegotiate on lower quantities to hedge your bets? How you make such decisions will be critical to your anti-fragile response to the future. Having some yardstick for such decision-making when the critical information is unclear may be the key to your survival or demise.

Who do you know 'on the ground'? With a need to keep the population calm in any a major emergency, official reports of the state of things may be 'optimistic' instead of 'realistic'. By contrast, some news outlets will highlight the negatives of a situation and you may respond unnecessarily to this negative information.

The people with whom you have developed relationships on the ground in each of your key localities will give you a clearer picture.

The Harvard Business Review of 27th Feb 2020 gives an example of the UPS hub in Kentucky being closed to all road traffic due an ice storm. Staff could not get to work sorting and dispatching – but the *airfield* was open – so workers were flown in from other cities. If you were the person in charge of that site had unilaterally responded to the initial media reports, there would have been unnecessary complications by pre-empting the creative company response to change the method of staff transportation to work.

Check with the local source. The local source told HQ the vital piece of information: the airport was open, but the roads were not. This is where having developed understanding of your complete supply-chain is vital – and where the power of relationships can be seen.

Map not just your suppliers but their suppliers – it may well be at that level that failure hits and cascades. This applies not just to their ability to remain in business, but their adherence to the ethics, regulations, and sourcing protocols your company requires and increasingly, that certain regulations and compliance now demand. Get this documented and then, in the words of the old Russian Proverb now quoted as being used memorably by Ronald Reagan : *Doveryai, no proveryai* – or to us in English:

*'Trust, but verify'.*

Early warning will give you access to alternatives before everyone else works out there is a problem, and before your sought-after commodities or services have escalated in price, if you can get them at all.

Several businesses with whom we work did such a check as soon as the possibility of a pandemic was reported. In one case, a product that was then procured in excess quantity of immediate need 'just in case' was later only able to be purchased *at a little over 60 times that price* – if you could get it at all.

Even more cautionary tales are those **of data breaches caused by third party vendors or suppliers** that impact your business and the personal information of your clients and employees. From a report on Vendor Risk Monitoring by Mitrotech:

- In 2023 a US telecommunications provider reportedly had a breach affecting customer data of more than 8 million customers. *What should alarm us in this case was that the bank had ceased the relationship with that cloud vendor six years previously.*
- There appears to have been no verification that the data held on their behalf had either been returned or deleted. A tricky one that. Hard to verify but at least there should be contractual sign off that this had been done. It at least gives a legal starting point of defence.
- This case comes back again to relationships. If you are in a sound customer relationship you should be able to be valued sufficiently that your point of contact *makes sure* that such a thing doesn't happen.
- In 2024 one of the largest sellers in the world of theatre and event tickets experienced such a loss: reportedly 560 MILLION customer data records were breached by a third party service provider.
- Similarly, also in 2024, a data warehouse was affected by a breach that affected 180 organisations using their services. This proved to be because of a lack of multifactor authorisation.

## Securing your critical component or commodity

Don't be like the accountant-led management of Kodak, who in March 1980 saw the falling price in the silver market and over-ruled the protestations of their Procurement Manager and insisted that he sell all his stock. He always kept a solid inventory of silver as it was the critical element in their whole film processing operation.  I know this because he had a close relationship with a client of mine, who was a client of his.

On the 27th March of that year this decision came home to roost. It was what became known as Silver Thursday – when the Hunt Brothers alleged efforts to manipulate the world supply of silver brought the whole market to its knees.

Kodak had to buy all of the silver stock back when it was at its most difficult to procure and at a rising price.

Given this background, it may be no surprise that Kodak didn't recognise the importance of digital photography.

This is even more amazing in that it was one of their employees, Steve Sasson, who invented the digital camera. It's not that Kodak did nothing about digital cameras. It is because they completely misunderstood the real benefits to the user and tried to make it a digital replica with the functionality of a film camera – making it too complicated

Kodak recovered from that and was the first to make it possible to move photos from camera to computer. Thereafter, they lost the trail of crumbs leading to Hansel and Gretel's safe house in the woods where the money could be counted – by totally missing the interrelationship of cameras and smart phones.

Check alternative and local suppliers and their capacity and suitability. Even if they are only occasionally used, but when needed are critical, at least review their status regularly  and keep the contact 'warm' – Black Swans eggs hatch in unlikely places.

**MARKET**
**Change before you have to:**
*Relevance of your products and/or services*
We have already addressed part of this when we thought about the core function of your business, but this is a time to seriously understand what is of priority to your customers in this world of tilting values and damaged political trust relationships.

In 'Value Merchants'[42], the authors, James. C. Anderson, Nirmalya Kumar, and James A. Narus make the important point that in their experience, despite there being only one reality, both customer and supplier have a different interpretation of it.

It is not an uncommon situation. So, we need to have those two interpretations converge in common meaning. How?  Old fashioned concept: talk to your customers.

---

[42] Value Merchants, James. C. Anderson, Nirmalya Kumar, and James A. Narus - My version printed in 2007

Pick up the phone (or if you can do so, actually go there and talk face to face) and check how they are getting along and what their immediate and foreseeable problems are.

The case of *all in this together* in dealing with current challenges gives a perfect opportunity to engage personally and find out what problems they are facing. Then use your knowledge of your own business and its expertise, experience, resources and relationships to suggest a way of addressing these. Failing that, just ask: "What can we do differently that would help you out?"

A survey is good but a telephone conversation makes the contact personal – especially when it comes from the top. You are saying that a client is important enough for you to pick up the phone or actually go there. Work from there and **don't delegate this**.

It is always easier to have someone buy than for you to sell. If a client tells you what they are facing and you can provide a solution, then you can describe what you think you can do and ask if that would be helpful.

A 30 minute conversation that has 10 minutes personal interaction to begin with and a 2 minutes close off, allows 18 minutes where you can refine the connection between the customer need and your services or goods - and together agree a workable plan forward that is better tailored to address your customer's needs.

After speaking to such a customer you can say with satisfaction: She just bought. The moral of the story is not to anticipate that your company's in-house interpretation of a client need is accurate.

### The milkshake market and the commuters

In 'Cognitive Surplus[43]: Creativity and generosity in a connected age', Clay Shirky gives the example of McDonalds planning their milkshake market extension.

In response to this initiative, within MacDonalds people started trying new formulae for different flavours.

The engineering and design teams looked at how better to mix the milkshake for optimal flavour and best profit.

However, one man sat in a McDonalds for a whole day and made a note of every milkshake sold - and who bought it - and when -and where they drank it.

Those *studying the milkshake as a product* missed what the person *studying people ordering milkshakes* learned: that it was the chosen 'breakfast-on-the-go' for commuters. Any other fast breakfast food meant handling something messy to eat. A milkshake is a reasonably good 'start-the-day' breakfast food AND is ideally packaged for the commuter.

*This knowledge would have otherwise been missed because it was not the usual way that people expected others to either drink a milkshake, or to have breakfast.*

---

43 Cognitive Surplus, Clay Shirky – My version printed in 2011

Perhaps your expectation of how your products or services are being used has moved on in a similar way without you noticing. Best check – but check where you get information – not opinion.

'Cognitive Surplus 'has a great line to remember:

*The faster you learn, the quicker you'll be able to adapt.*

Shirky points out that behaviours change. What used to be a 'customer need' may have changed in character quite significantly – and as we have seen, in some cases at light speed.

To demonstrate the reasons behind some of those changes, Shirky uses the example of remembering telephone numbers. In the past we learned them because we needed to, not because it was something we always wished we could do. Once that need was removed – so also has disappeared our telephone-number-remembering capacity.

Don't let your company go the way of a no-longer-remembered telephone number.

Cognitive Surplus is a great little book. Mine was printed in 2011 and for most of its life lived in the Kensington and Chelsea library in London before being deemed to be what a colleague of mine, known for her malapropisms , would have called *'super flewous to rekwi ments'*. No longer accorded shelf space, the book was released to the second-hand book trade – and to me. Another example of The Long Tail in action – we second-hand bookshop aficionados keep books in circulation long after publishers think they are dead. We'll come back later to the wisdom of this little book.

## Immediately identifiable risks and opportunities
### *Tourism and hospitality*

In her truly impressive and meticulously researched book 'Overbooked: the exploding business of travel and tourism' , Elizabeth Becker paints a real but daunting picture of what the industry has done to the magical places that are the source of its content.

Becker is a travel journalist and 'Overbooked[44]' is wonderfully descriptive but yet fact-filled as it presents the reality of our impact. This is a call for a universal standard of ethics and protocols throughout the industry before we lose cultural identity in a grand homogenisation, and irreparably damage the environment as we do so.

Elizabeth Becker's 'Overbooked' factually notes the real impact of what until recently was the invisible – or at least unattended – tourism segment of each of our economies.

Sadly, much of the destruction our passion for travel has caused has been underwritten by governments. Before the pandemic, citizens of some of the most visited cities and once pristine areas of the world had already had enough and started to protest that there was no more room for locals and that we are destroying the very things we came to see because they are treasured.

---

[44] Overbooked: the exploding business of travel and tourism, Elizabeth Becker - Written in 2013 and my paperback version printed in 2016

Since the world reopened these protests have expanded. They expanded in defence of a way of life threatened by being swamped by people who do not share the values, care, and appreciation of the environment that is the heritage and pride of the locals they came to visit.

The old model of tourism well describe in 'Overbooked' was extremely flawed. This is a chance to rethink this and many other sector models and apply more sensitive values. Many destinations are doing just this – noticeably Venice and Amsterdam, who are both working with their local communities to return their cities to the locals and redress the previous imbalances and excesses.

This trend will accelerate as new models emerge – but for the destinations where tourism is a major part of their local economy, it will be a focus of a different sort.

Mexico's tourism sector supports over 4 million people, 93% of whom are in companies of fewer than 10 employees. This vital group will find benefit from a radical and sudden shift in tourism destination choice since travelling to the USA has become fraught with border-control risk in early 2025. According to a Times of India article of March 2025, the USA has been one of the top three most visited countries in the world with over 79.3 million visitors. But tourism in the USA is already registering a significant reduction.

In a 2024 report[45] the USA was cited by the World Travel and Tourism Council (WTTC) as having a staggering

---

[45] World Travel and Tourism Council (WTTC) 2024 Economic Impact Trend Report

$2.36 Trillion value – stated to be 2.97% of the country's GDP. The US data analysis firm YouGov reported in April 2025 that 35% of international travellers surveyed were discouraged from visiting the US, while Mexico was becoming a destination of choice.

If your business is associated with or impacted by tourism in any way – tighten your seat belts, because the downward slope seems to be accelerating. Just the loss of the Canadian tourist dollar will be significant for companies in the USA – and not just those who are directly involved in tourism. According to the U.S. Travel Association these tourists spend $20.5 billion and support 140,000 American jobs.

### Does tourism impact your business?

If you think tourism has nothing to do with your business, think again. At the time of writing of 'Overbooked', the industry was valued at $7.6 trillion of the world economy, employing one in eleven people. In 2024, the World Travel and Tourism Council reported that 10% of all economic activity was tourism related and that the industry accounted for 357 million jobs worldwide.

Is this relevant to your business? It may well be.

In Australia, in the region where I was the Economic Development and Tourism Manager, we conducted an informal study of the dribble-down effect of the tourism dollar on the local economy. By tracking impacts we were

---

able to demonstrate how widely the general economy is linked to that of tourism.

Take a small example: a medium sized bakery that saw a 45% drop in daily business from the impact of a city-based travel agency closure - because the staff no longer bought sandwiches, ordered special occasion cakes, etc. That in turn affected the supply chain of the local egg producer, the service people who looked after commercial kitchen equipment, the transport company bringing regular supplies.

A coral reef scuba diving company's supply chain reached back to Italy for its tanks and regulators, and was dependent upon land transport to the marina (purchase and servicing of vehicles and employment of drivers and mechanics), boat transport to the reef marina fees, fuel purchase, onboard luncheon catering supplies, scuba tank and equipment maintenance and certification services, engine servicing, printers for certificates, training companies to certify guides.

Considering the layering of the tourism industry and its impacts on its supply chain, it may well cross over that of your business.

Without the underpinning mass previously borne by tourism, what will be the impact on production of the supplies critical for your business in the dribble-down effect?

Displacement of one in ten of the global workforce has further impacts that don't need spelling out. Belt tightening will be an under-statement. If you are based in the USA, the tourism and hospitality industries will impact your business in ways yet not revealed – so build your bamboo scaffolding soundly as you plan the future.

If you are outside the USA what opportunities does this offer? Portugal, Mexico and the country of Georgia have offered Digital Nomad visas. Universities outside the USA – notably UK, Germany, Australia and the Netherlands are seeing increasing foreign student enrolments.

Are there trade shows or symposiums that can be offered and that you can host or where you can showcase your services?

If your primary market has been the USA and tariffs now make that problematic, how can you rapidly promote your services and products in other markets?

Entering new geographies has its challenges but it also offers huge opportunities.

In working with one company in the business of water purification and treatment, we isolated one of their un-noticed assets. They handled all the water treatment for rehabilitative water therapies for the horses of a royal household. That is a pretty sound level of credibility and instead of focusing on the more completive areas of their market, this proved a valuable market-entry point in developing new territories. From there they were able to expand on the basis of that credibility carrying over to their more traditional offerings.

New value chains will emerge. They always do – but the pain of the intermediate period will stretch beyond the immediate impact on the main players of the travel industry.

*The best journeys in life are those*
*that answer questions you never thought to ask.*

Rich Ridgeway

# CHAPTER THREE
## The rise in valuing Values

*Values are like fingerprints.*
*Nobodies are the same*
*but you leave them all over everything you do.*

Elvis Presley

### Values and authenticity

It was in 1924, at the time of writing 101 years ago, that Lord Chief Justice Hewart made a ruling that has been universally abbreviated.

That ruling was made at the superior court of England and Wales and that of many Commonwealth countries at was then called 'The King's Bench', now a division of the High Court. The context pertained to the independence and impartiality of national judges appointed to the Permanent Court of International Justice.

Our commonly used abbreviation is:

*Justice must not only be done, but be seen to be done.*

The actual ruling was even more adamant:

*Justice should not only be done,*
***but should manifestly and undoubtedly***
*be seen to be done.*

It is an interesting aside in light of our times that an article in the Adelaide Law Review in 2016 discussing this ruling argues that in the wider context of impartiality *" the appearance of justice is better promoted by judges who are reflective of the community they are appointed to serve".*

I mention this ruling because if you claim values, they must be authentic – and you cannot 'magic up' authenticity. 'To be seen to be done', they must have been, or should be measured.

The results of you acting on your values needs to be accurately recorded if you are one of the many companies aligning to the global shift in Values Accounting – or making legitimate what in many instances in the past were unsubstantiated 30 second sound bites.

In the context of the times at the time of writing the first edition of this book, I asked Hary Olaru, VP for the IBM Business Services Centers in Europe to share his view of the unfortunate situation in the US following the death of George Floyd that was causing massive protests and aggressive reactions. He pointed out that although this surfaced in the US, such happenings occur throughout Europe and in every country and when they do, history has demonstrated that changes in mindset ensue.

I quote part of his response directly: "irrespective of the role one plays in the society, ...(we should) always keep in mind the importance of treating each other with equality, openness and respect".

Hary then related his personal experience of the communist regime overthrow in his native Romania (with over 1,000 deaths). This was responsive to how, despite the supposed basis of communism being to make everyone equal, reality had demonstrated that in this version of socialism some people were more equal than others.

This has resonance for us all in whatever country we reside.

Hary Olaru then listed a remarkable record of IBM. It is a record that shows that IBM has historically been ahead of the curve, and gives validity to the company's current championing of diversity and fairness.

In the first two examples, the company was not yet named IBM, but it seems the philosophy of the later so named company had its base here:

In 1899 - the first African-American employee hired
In 1914 - the first employee with disability
In 1943 - the first woman VP.
In 1946 the first African-American Sales rep
In 1947 - the first African-American software engineer. This was a first not just at IBM, but in America: John Stanley Ford was his name, and this was well before the 1963 Civil Rights Act.

I am grateful for the chance to include Hary's views here. Such beliefs have meaning beyond time or corporate environment. In promoting these, it makes me a part of what I call in my earlier book 'Shrapnel Free Explosive

Growth', the 'unpaid marketing force' that gets your message out effectively - with more validity by being third party.

However, I must disclaim that I am not a truly impartial commentator on IBM. Before becoming a consultant on business strategy to global companies, governments, and non-profits, my Dad was a successful IBMer winning attendance at many "100 Per cent Club" events, and S.E. Asia Divisional Head.

Further, I have the rare distinction of having Thomas Watson Jr. riding in our small family car on an Australian bush picnic when I was a child. When an emu pacing beside the car caused our Labrador- cross- cattle-dog to leap over both me and my brother, headed for the open window on Mr. Watson's side, with great presence of mind he grabbed the animal mid-air and travelled to the next stopping point with a quivering, whimpering 30kilos (about 66lbs) of excited black fur in his lap.

Even as a child I recognised Thomas Watson Jr. as a genuinely open person, lacking any airs of superiority. He was later to be voted one of the 100 most influential people of the 20th century. An IBM employee booklet that describes its personnel principles has on its cover a 1962 quote by Thomas Watson Jr. that has resonance for us all:

*I believe the real difference between success and failure in a corporation can very often be traced to the question of how well the organisation brings out the great energies and talents of its people.*

But I digress.

I find it interesting to note that Hary's comments are not part of a global IBM 'Aren't we good chaps' campaign. Like the examples I mention about Southwest – they are more powerful for travelling on the' influence underground'.

*In making the values of your company broadcast, it is often in the smallest things that they come to be amplified.*

I recall Michael Dell being interviewed – at last – by Gartner in one of their leader interviews. Several times Michael had alluded to 'when he came back to be interviewed again in 20 years time' – alluding to this omission over the last 20 years.

Finally, the interviewer responded and asked that should Michael be back in 20 years, what would he like to be known for over that intervening period.

You know, I truly cannot remember the end of the responding sentence - but I shall never forget how the answer began – I was so impressed with it that I never recalled the rest. It began like this:

After a thoughtful pause, Michael Dell said: "I think we would like to be remembered for…"

**WE** would like to be remembered for….

It was totally unconscious – demonstrating a lifelong philosophy in so few words.

A former HP colleague of mine and former Product Manager whom I hold in very high esteem was headhunted to Dell. She later told me that she loved going to work– and went on to say with a laugh that she never thought she would say those words in the same sentence. You can see why.

Your company would probably like *you* to say in the future: "In 2025 and in the extra-ordinary years that followed – **WE** were able to...." I hope such a statement will come quite naturally after your Swivel.

The refocus of your company needs to be based on its own principles. That refocus should be in authentic ways meaningful to your staff and your clients - and should support a better future society, with fair rewards to all.

How do you demonstrate that you have fulfilled your value commitments if you cannot record them effectively? Do so.

**Unquoing the status quo**
The biggest obstacle others found in moving to a values-recording discipline in any organisation is the inertia of the status quo.

In 'Unstoppable[46]: Finding Hidden Assets to renew the core and fuel profitable growth', Chris Zook points out the dangers of the status quo because it offers what appears to

---

[46] Unstoppable Finding Hidden Assets to renew the core and fuel profitable growth, Chris Zook  - My copy printed in 2007

be shelter from the storm, but as he writes with prescience: *"what if the storm never ends?"*

I am indebted to the blog 'Coordination Freedom ' that alerted me to the origin of the much repeated partial quotation of the term *'tyranny of the status quo'* by Milton Friedman. The full original citation is as follows:

*There is enormous inertia*
**-a tyranny of the status quo—**
*in private and especially governmental arrangements.*
*Only a crisis—actual or perceived— produces real change.*

According to the article on the blog, this appeared in the 1982 preface of Milton Friedman's book 'Capitalism and Freedom'. Friedman then continued to alert us to something that we should factor into our future planning:

*When that crisis occurs, the actions that are taken depend on the ideas that are lying around.*

The sudden global shift of 2025 is a catalyst to un-quo the status, so searching for those ideas lying around in your own organisation is paramount. They are usually found in plain sight but may have been intentionally obscured by people who prefer the status quo – possibly because it relieves them from decision making – or so they think, until a crisis prevails.

If you move the furniture around in your assessment you will be pleasantly surprised by some of the building blocks of the future hidden behind heavy outdated practices and methods that have been fiercely protected.

## Creative window dressing

Attending a forum in Manchester in 2005 or 2006 where Richard Florida was the Keynote speaker, during question time I challenged the lip-service statements of the then Central Government Minister responsible for economic development of the regions of the UK.

I cited the case of huge financial incentives given a global corporation with peppercorn rental in one of the prime real estate locations in Liverpool in one of what are known there as 'The Three Graces', the beautiful Liver, Cunard, and Port of Liverpool buildings on the banks of the River Mersey. The Minister had claimed that this style of government support generated jobs.

In this case, I challenged, these were not the 300 jobs claimed. There were possibly 30 people employed full time – the balance were temporary workers - and furthermore, the non-complying work practices of the company receiving these benefits were regularly sanitised for a display to the contrary with each advance notice that inspectors were due. So what had been financed were not new jobs, but a subsidy to ensure a poorly skilled workforce has no advancement opportunities - and no chance to object or they would never find more temporary work from agencies catering to the corporations concerned.

I asked the rhetorical question: "What could have been accomplished by investing that money to identify, develop, and champion the creativity of every one of those temporary workers?" I was so angry my voice was shaking when I added: "In Liverpool, for heaven's sake!"

# SWIVEL

Richard came off the stage at the end and sought me out like a heat-seeking missile to say this was exactly what he was trying to get across and thank me for raising it in the public forum.

From this encounter I discussed with him the opportunity to work with us in the locality where at the time I was the Cultural Strategy Manager tasked with putting culture back into the planning regulations for the doubling of the city – planning guidelines and budgets for which had previously disappeared.

Richard Florida was willing – but I came up against the status quo - which proved an immovable force.

In the same locality the now world-famous designer Thomas Heatherwick had previously held a post as 'artist-in-residence', but in all his time there could not secure any commission to employ his creative talent.

When we met in Heatherwick Studios in London some years later, he lamented that the main thing he had accomplished was to *stop* bureaucrats from doing things, not for making a design contribution.

I told him how important it was that he did stop the unravelling of character of a place studied internationally as a successful 'new town' despite national cultural cringe about its 'differentness'.

At that time, the city worthies seemed still eager to make it into an ordinary – and therefore familiar -British town.  Presumably, their familiarity with that model meant that one could adopt traditional practice and not have to re-think options and make difficult decisions.

Thomas was prepared to undertake a new commission there – he held an affinity with the place - but try as I might – the status quo prevailed.

With his growing international recognition there is no way Thomas could now be afforded for those purposes. That creativity found outlets in designing Little Island in New York, Al Fayah Park in Abu Dhabi, the new Routemaster buses for London, the Olympic cauldron of parts for the 2020 Olympics (that made a visual statement of the contribution of each country that together makes the whole), and Google campus in Mountain View California.

Some years later I heard that a senior Councillor said that they now recognised what changes I had been trying to encourage - they just weren't ready for it then, but were now. The moment of opportunity to harness willing talent of such character had passed – although no doubt there is more willing talent always there to be encouraged to contribute.

### The value of diversity
*In companies and in localities*
*– creativity and diversity of thinking are under-valued.*
*It is time this stopped.*

*It denies us access to richer thinking about the elements that make what we do and where we do it worthwhile and pleasurable, as well as providing expected functionality.*

At the time of writing the first edition of this book, following the universal horror at the death in Minneapolis of George Floyd that released the pent up anger of decades of institutional discrimination in communities throughout the U.S.A. and elsewhere in the world, companies advertised their stated policy of zero tolerance for any sort of racist or discriminatory behaviour in their companies.

The fact that this needs to be stated shows how far we have drifted from what, in an ideal world, should be the norm.

*There is value in diversity and we have undervalued it.*

In 'The Rise of the Creative Class[47], Richard Florida's research demonstrated how localities that value diversity become magnets for talent. The same holds for companies.

The survey results on which Florida's book is based identify how diverse lifestyles such as those of the LGBT community underpinned the localities attracting the most creative talent. Such acceptance allowed people who think differently to live happily within communities where the views and preferences of others are part of a richness of input to solutions and to community building.

This valuing of diversity was stronger than any government incentive and Florida argues still – in his many speaking engagements and subsequent books, for creating societies where we harvest the creativity of everyone.

---

[47] The Rise of the Creative Class, Richard Florida - my well-used version printed in 2004

As I pointed out to a couple of people who came to scold me for hiring a particular individual in the company, his job required exactly the sort of personality characteristics that were those to which they objected.

I pointed out that this was a role none of us would consider – or be considered suitable to deliver – and furthermore – that if we only hired people just like us we would either all be bouncing off the walls, or be exceptionally boring.

The Harvard Business Review calls it 'Cognitive Diversity.' No surprise then, that they report that research demonstrates that companies with such diversity registered higher market valuations.

*In such companies, employees valued what they called 'intense internal competition' as well as collaboration – not seeing any conflict in having both.*

There is an interesting allusion to Stanley Crouch in the book 'Circle of Innovation' by Tom Peters. Putting a focus on diversity and the long history of civil and women's rights in many countries, Crouch made a statement that is worth incorporating into our own thinking as we plan.

*When you look at things solely in terms of race or class, you miss what is really going on.*

To put this in context, Stanley Crouch is poet, jazz musician, music and cultural critic, mentor and friend to jazz and classical musician Wynton Marsalis, and once a civil right activist who previously supported the Black

Power movement of the late 1960s. However, this support led to disillusionment and resulted in his more open, less 'one issue' thinking in relation to such movements and the issues to which they respond.

*A single issue focus is never the way to the best resolution – whether on diversity or anything else.*

When you and your team **Swivel** – think about root causes to broaden the issues you see. Then you can isolate where your business can fill useful gaps in the 'need' equation.

### The values shift

The fact that values needed to be revisited was already writ large by the global nature of the crisis of Covid-19. There was immediate and comprehensive understanding by most, that we truly *are all in this together,* and that personal responsibility extends to protecting others by our own actions.

As witness, even the major oil companies decided that the post pandemic world needs to rethink values as was reported by Technology Editor, Judy Feder in the Journal of Petroleum Technology on 1st June, 2020. She records the announcement of ambitious climate change initiatives by the French multinational oil and gas company *Total*, joining *Shell, BP,* and *Repsol* who had previously acted in a similar manner in response to sustainability goals.

For those who say shareholders demand profit above all else – it would appear not – or at least – not now.  The shares in *Total* rose by 6% immediately following the announcement.

Despite "Drill baby Drill", what is known as "Big Oil" is in no rush at the time of writing, to do so. There are many reasons, not the least of which is that overproduction has cost the industry before – and there is capacity in existing refineries and high costs to develop new ones.

One cannot predict how the removal of sustainability targets and diversity policies, will play out. However a Springer article[48] in June 2024 has this to say: "Polluting businesses that perform very well in terms of ESG metrics have higher worker productivity, better financial performance, lower organizational risk, and less information asymmetry".

**An example of possibilities from Scandinavia:**
The Norwegian based agribusiness firm Yara committed $25million to provide food for more than 1 million people in Southern and Eastern Africa where the impacts of Covid- risked leaving vast swathes of hunger and deprivation.

Not only that, in recognition of the need to grow, harvest, and transport food in locations of deprivation needs support, they have targeted certain other efforts.

---

[48] Springer:Assessing the impact of ESG scores on market performance in polluting companies: a post-COVID-19 analysis  https://rdcu.be/ekDdS

- In Myanmar when the recently harvested watermelon crop lost its China market during lockdown, the company purchased the whole crop and donated the watermelons to three local hospitals.
- In Colombia, food transport was allowable travel under lockdown but drivers were unable to get meals en route, so upon arrival with their load, all delivery drivers were offered a free lunch or dinner.
- In North America, crops unable to be sold during the pandemic were bought directly from farmers by food banks that are heavily supported by the company.

I offer this example because the type of disruption to farming that current tariffs have caused /will cause, may mean your communities need this type of support and this is something you should factor into planning. Not just your survival but that of the network of small businesses and agricultural enterprises that make up our communities.

*The landscape is now defined by values.*
Does this change of thinking have relevance for your company? How can your company be a leader, an innovator, and a darned good global citizen?

There is a vital element of such a values- based restatement of business purpose. It relies on supporting actions – and often requires revisions of existing arrangements to give them authenticity.

While values should always underpin your cause just for the *value* of that value, and not be there for window-dressing, they can also identify new opportunities within the marketplace as well. These may well extend your current portfolio of goods and services as you recognise, and respond to, new priorities in this fast changing and radically transformed world.

In 'The Long Tail', author Chris Anderson makes the following statement that has relevance in its original context of being about new markets – but it also has bearing on the subject of values.

*In a world of infinite choice, context – not content, is king.*

### Four values highlighted by the Covid-19 crisis

According to a report by Delphine Gibassier on 2nd May, 2020 in 'Ethical Corporation', since around 2010 more than 300 new types of Value Recording Accounting Models have been trialled globally. Gibassier identifies four current corporate values being tracked. Let's examine them:

### Intellectual Capital

The article states that fewer than 50% of companies report on Intellectual Capital. However in the analysis the need to respond to crisis demonstrated the value and power of R&D, company culture, and relevant information systems as the underpinning for the reorganisation and scale-up for response.

### Social Capital

Social capital has demonstrated that is people and their social connections that are the glue to keep things together and to find new ways of doing things.

During Covid, the most northerly communities in the United Kingdom in the Shetland Islands were unable to source PPE equipment. After an online design was published, fabulously creative scrubs appeared at the hospitals, reputedly resulting in great competition to have the scrubs made out of children's sheeting starring super heroes.

There are examples of the importance of this type of social value from around the world:  industry cluster groups working together to support their weaker members - and arts, music and dance groups  keeping morale high -  like the street in Wales that started each lockdown day with a dance in the streets, dancing together from driveways and in cul-de-sacs.

Similarly, the balcony wine parties of Italy, and over-the-fence wine parties in France.

It is Social Capital that is the glue of community - and community is where innovation thrives.

### *Biodiversity*
The development of prohibitive laws and their strict enforcement can only work with global pressures – and global corporations and all companies can lead that by changing their own policies.

The UN Conference on Trade and Development writes of the importance of making adherence to Voluntary Sustainability Standards a core element of supply chain purchasing agreements. This goes back to the earlier point about checking your supply chain's supply chain and its sustainability – not just in terms of their economic viability.

### Human Capital

Within the organisation we should rethink who our most 'valuable' employees are. That means understanding the benefit to the individual. It means understanding how people informally communicate and connect to get things done, and of understanding previously unidentified pinch points being relieved by individual (and sometimes team) effort.

Two useful methods of encapsulating these new value objectives as you restructure can be found at Future Fit Business *(not the fitness training website)*, Doughnut Economics, and The Circular Economy Collage. There are many others but let's start with these to give some sense of the objective, the methods of implementation, the benefits, and the legitimate measurement of outcome.

Future Fit Foundation in the UK has developed guidelines available under a Creative Commons licence. If you go to *futurefitbusiness.org/benchmark-documents* you can download them from here. It is a bit circuitous, so go to Page 46 of the Methodology guide to see how your business can benefit. You can read about Doughnut Economics[49] at *kateraworth.com/doughnut/*. The French initiative Circular Economy Collage has workshops in several languages for the cost of a small donation.

---

[49] http://www.ethicalcorp.com/we-need-radically-different-accountancy-value-companies-post-pandemic-world

# SWIVEL

Warren Buffet's mentor, Ben Graham, has a quote that is worth us taking to heart:

*In the short run the market is a voting machine
but in the long run it is a weighing machine*

# CHAPTER FOUR
## The bend in the road ahead

*A bend in the road is not the end of the road...unless you fail to make the turn.*

Helen Keller

Having made your assessment of the current state of your business, go back and list separately your 'Wobble Points' and 'Building Blocks'.

Before taking action on any Wobble Point get your team together to review the options. The very thing that seems to be creating an impediment may have functionality in another style of operation, for a different client (even those only identified generically), or when combined with something else, create improvement of opportunity for new sales.

**Potential Wobble Points**
Bain and Company report that from conversations with a wide range of CEOs, the message from each was the same – and it is threefold:

- The way things were is something to which we cannot return –and must not return.
- Talk with your most important customers immediately.

- Let the company ethos and values be the guide to every decision.

If that held for the post-pandemic SWIVEL – it should be strongly endorsed for the global-shift SWIVEL.

So where you find a 'Wobble Point', consider all three points in your potential evaluation.

At the same time, as you assess, make a note of every issue that arises. This list can provide guidelines and warnings that ensure that your future policies and methods allow for their resolution within your bamboo scaffolding framework of ethos and values.

Such 'Danger Ahead' indications can provide similar guidance to protect you from impacts from the arrival of any future Black Swan.

Don't forget as you assess that some Black Swans are bred in-house. Pretend it's Easter and make it an honour point for anyone who finds a Black Swan's egg within your structure, or your supply chain, or regulatory environment.

Keep an egg tally.

Make it visible, personal, and reward well every one that is found.

Perhaps beside your egg tally you can have an Incubator tally. That would show which egg was dealt with in which way – and the outcome. Such things can take the edge off the urgency you may be facing as the world shifts and markets shudder in response.

These ways of keeping track of the reality within your organisation are not superfluous. They change the tone and they inspire the hunt for more eggs and drive creativity with incubator solutions.

What you are doing is what was advised in 'Hope is Not a Method': building in flexibility *(and what Taleb would call antifragility)* so that you are **not surprised by being surprised** - so that *'when the unexpected occurs, response is prompt, action is deliberate, and the organization stays on course'.*

The authors point out something that can frame your response to creating this map of 'how we did it' and overlying it with one of 'how we now must do it'.

*The paradox in creating the future*
*is that you cannot predict the future.*
*Success will come from being able*
*to accommodate the unexpected,*
*exploiting opportunity and working through setbacks.*

In this context the Egg Tally and the Incubator take on new resonance.

### Location
Can you afford to stay in the same location as now?

Jonathan Boyar, writing in Forbes[50] about hidden assets and how to find them, gives the example of the

---

[50] https://www.forbes.com/sites/jonathanboyar/2019/02/12/value-understanding-hidden-assets/#67fc38fe5bfd

Tiffany's Building in Manhattan. The cost of running the building may have been a concern for them too, but perhaps you might benefit from a rethink if similar circumstances apply.

In the USA, GAAP (Generally Accepted Accounting Practices) requires real estate to be valued at its historical cost irrespective of appreciation. This meant that the Tiffany's *Building* ended up being worth more than the whole Tiffany's portfolio.

The equivalent to GAAP is IFRS (International Financial reporting standards). This is used in most of Europe, Latin America, Asia, and parts of Africa. Countries using IFRS include EU members, Australia, Canada, Brazil, South Africa, South Korea, and India (slightly modified and called Ind AS). After Brexit, the UK equivalent adopted in 2021 is a replica of that it used to be under the EU, but with the caveat that it may be later modified.

Wherever you live, this principle may be worth investigating.

Wobble Points can include some common misconceptions you find as you ***Swivel***. `In 'Management and Machiavelli[51]: Power and Authority in Business Life'.

---

[51] Management and Machiavelli[51]: Power and Authority in Business Life, Antony Jay - My copy printed in 1988 gifted to my Dad in 1989

The author (now Sir) Antony Jay suggests these two are common:
- over and underestimating the strength of your capability,
- the inability to meet changed quality or capacity requirements.

## Possible Building Blocks

As you **Swivel**, you will notice things that may have always been there but now seem to invite further investigation for application in new ways or in new markets. As Clay Shirky notes in 'Cognitive Surplus' you need to:

> *identify new opportunities linked to old motives via the right incentives.*

### *New or familiar?*

As you assess the relevance of what you find and as you seek your place in the market of the currently changing world, bear in mind the refinement of definition made in 'Hope is Not a Method':

> *There is a very real difference between something truly new and that which is unfamiliar.*

If your possible building block is truly new – it will lead you down a different path than that which is merely unfamiliar. Both may have valid and profitable outcomes – but be clear in your definition so that when you evaluate the market and your entrance to it with the creation built with your building blocks, you do so appropriately.

'New' will have different challenges from those of an adaptation of the familiar, no matter how elegantly 'different' you think that to be.

### Define your own R words

In the same book the authors caution about the 'easy-fix' attraction of employing the buzz word methods of 'Reshaping, Re-engineering, Re-inventing, and Re-positioning'.

You may wish to do some of any or all of the above – but define your own. The 'off-the-shelf' versions were made for a world that doesn't exist anymore. As Alvin Toffler says in 'Previews and Premises':

> *what passes for 'advanced thinking' amounts to no more than swapping obsolete models.*

Any of the 're' factors you decide to create or employ should be tailor-made and fit with your company ethos.

### Isolating what makes 'you' special

As you identified 'Building Blocks', what part of them comprised the 'you' in your offer– a 'you' that extends a particularly different aspect to that offered by the general product or service that is your core?

I think it is indicative of an era we *shouldn't* emulate, that in the 2007 printing of my version of 'Mobilizing Minds', Lowell L. Bryan and Claudia I. Joyce promote what appears to be a then popular McKinsey model of 'Collaborative Leadership'.

From my reading of this, it is a case of putting shinier wheels on an old model instead of rethinking its whole design. This model recommends a 'top 20 leaders' collaboration: in other words – a variation on organisational hierarchy.

This brings an interesting point of consideration in terms of what a consultant knows that your own people don't.

As an example, McKinsey advised ENRON for over 15 years and the ENRON CEO was ex-McKinsey.

McKinsey also advised Purdue Pharma (The name Purdue coming from that of the family name of one of the founders, not the university) on how to accelerate sales of OxyContin. This allegedly despite knowledge that the claim that it worked in the first 12 hours and still advising doctors to increase the dose – increasing addiction. The drug itself showed no increased benefit over other drugs on the market, but the result of this aggressive marketing has seen it leading the opioid addiction figures. The company reached a final settlement with the court of $7.4bn. McKinsey agreed to pay $650 million. The people affected are a tragic legacy.

I could continue with the list of McKinsey advice that proved costly and certainly there are many worthwhile consultancies. I work for one. I make the point to be cautious about who you trust to offer advice on the company you run and for which you have responsibility for its success.

Unlike the McKinsey recommendation of involving 'top 20 leaders', **Swivel** suggests that you need to flatten the hierarchy, and that there is no point in limiting collaborative input to any randomly selected number of people, especially as in this McKinsey model 'worthy' people. (Being part of the Boy's Club was never any guarantee of creative thinking or sage forward thinking.

Added to that, in times of re-evaluation refocus, the concept of *organising* networks under a 'Network Manager' seems almost ludicrous.

What we want is a company full of solution-oriented people who create their own networks under natural leadership.

That leadership drives from deep knowledge of some vital aspect of the tools that allow the network to push forward vigorously outside traditional structures. In other words, they find their bit of the bamboo scaffolding where collectively they can restructure it with new types of lashing that make the whole stronger.

*"We are all in this together"* has long been the case – but traditional models of company organisation have limited input to those who are probably the most ill-placed to know the real mechanics and lubrication of the wheels upon which their company moves forward.

### Less is more
Don't be enticed into adding anything that detracts from the simplicity of your offer - unless it adds real value.

## *Waste: One man's rubbish is another man's treasure*

Essentially, the Apollo 13 problem was one about the effective use – or discarding – of a by-product.

What by- products do you have that could be useful in other sectors or applications?

In my book 'Shrapnel Free Explosive Growth' I give the example of leaders in the petrochemical industry who were very familiar with each other after years of sitting around tables discussing things pertinent to the sector. In this case I was leading the development of a strategy where these competing companies identified where it made sense to work collaboratively so all ships would rise, and planned forward actions to do so.

One gentleman arrived late and apologised that they had just finished a production run for which the by-product had to be rapidly disposed of. He had encountered some hiccups in doing so, and these had delayed him.

The executive who led the company that was located literally next door to the one of the newly arrived person pushed his chair back in amazement. He exclaimed that this was the same product they had a need for in one of their products. For years they had it shipped down the Mississippi River to New Orleans at due cost and inconvenience – not knowing they could have got it at a great price and with ease from next door.

### Mosaics of small victories

In 'Thick Face, Black Heart, my version printed in 1992, author Chin-Ning Chu points out the benefit of taking the bits of your wins and failures and building a winner's podium from them. As the book points out:

> *Success in life often comes from accumulating a*
> *stronghold of small victories.*
> *Failure is often caused by overlooking insignificant events.*

### No longer fit for purpose function or process

Does this mean you discard it? Before you do, evaluate what qualities the function performed and whether it did so well. If it did perform well for something no longer relevant to your company, what are the positive elements that can be adapted for use elsewhere – not necessarily in your company? To do this examine the functionalities and find who needs them and if yours are suitable or could be, for different use.

### Discard or adapt another

In Seattle, Washington and surrounding King County, old processes for Emergency Services First Responders were discarded in favour of an adaption of one from a 'parallel world'; an adaptation of the motorsport 'Pit Crew' methods.

Adaptation of these methods to dealing with sudden cardiac arrest has resulted in a more than 50% survival rate. Now, all Emergency Services Responders have standard expectations of what needs to be done, how, and in what order of priority. After every incident they follow what they call a G-A-S process *(Gather-Analyze-*

*Summarize)* and review the whole incident based on particular pieces of information so they can continually improve.

The common denominator in using a Pit Lane approach?

*The functionality*: Time related, urgent decision-making.

### Find new uses elsewhere

Can you licence and certify an outstanding methodology? Your processes or functionality may not be as spectacular or as well respected externally (yet) as pit crew performance in motorsports, but may still be able to be packaged as a product for use elsewhere.

Fraunhofer Institute for Industrial Engineering in Stuttgart has developed a clever method of analysing what they call the 'Invisible Web' – invisible to us but not to global researchers reviewing research papers that amongst other things reveal future trends.

By breaking down the component functionalities of a low performing product and searching for mention of the need for such capabilities/functionalities, they have revealed some startling and rather substantial new markets for components that were originally designed for quite different purposes. Contact me if this has relevance for you.

### Your star attraction no longer a star?

Change the stage.

Rebecca Sentence writes about some clever accompanies that did just that in her blog on *econsultancy.com*. Take *Goats2Meeting*[52] for example. Up-state New York 'Sweet Farm' non-profit animal sanctuary saw its funding streams come to an abrupt halt with no visitors to their in-person animal experiences during Covid. This working farm rescues and rehabilitates farm animals, and plants and promotes over 300 heritage crops

As an alternative funding stream, they started *Goats2Meeting* where a company could pay to have a goat, llama, or some other farm animal make an appearance on a company team call to liven up the 'work-at-home' experience.

Initial offerings between $95 (10 min) and $250 (20 min) for a virtual farm visitor for an unlimited number of online meeting participants, to a longer tour, or for a special animal cameo, proved so popular that they introduced a bonus VIP tour for a $750 donation.

If, in the current shifted world order your star is a product that is no longer as useful as it was, dust off the glitter and examine the creature beneath.

### The things in the cupboard under the stairs
You know the ones – all those things that are still in the company but are metaphorically stuffed into spare corners because they are no longer useful - and this metaphorical

---

[52] https://www.sweetfarm.org/virtual-visits

cupboard under the stairs isn't the home of a young magician.

In 'Unstoppable', Chris Zook reminds us that it was from things lying about that the lifesaving workaround that saved the Apollo 13 mission was put together.

When the famous message: "Houston. We have a problem" was received at Mission Control, the people who had the unenviable task of working out a solution could only use things already aboard the spacecraft to fit a round hose into a square hole with no leakage – and solve the problem of excessive $CO_2$ caused by a problem in the 'scrubbers' meant to trap the excess $CO_2$. Without a solution the crew would be poisoned before their return to earth.

As has often been said in relation to the term 'The Force', it is really duct tape that holds most things together – and in this case it was duct tape plus space suit hose for connecting, together with plastic bags and a funnel made from the cardboard covers of log books, that built the life-saving solution.

As with every 'Wobble Point', the first step was to define the problem precisely. The next was to get a list of everything that was on board – the 'Building Blocks' available. Then, they could design a 'work-around' creatively employing whatever was available within the space ship to fit a round peg into a square hole - with no leakage.

Maybe you should make an inventory like this and see if new thinking and a ***Swivel*** perspective can find new, useful and lucrative uses as you build your antifragile successful future company.

*Inspiration is everywhere*
*once you specifically define the problem to be solved.*

While we are in space, consider how science fiction caused the cell (mobile) phone to be developed. The website *destination-innovation.com*[53] tells the story of how ex-US Navy Motorola engineer and Star Trek fan Martin 'Marty' Cooper developed the prototype mobile phone in 1973.

Reputedly, Marty was concerned with the influence that their competitor AT&T was exerting to secure from the FCC a dedicated air wave frequency for their car phones – which were mobile only in that they were installed in cars and were as mobile as the vehicle.

Instead of competing head on, Marty's team rethought the whole mobility issue with phones.

Fascinated with Captain Kirk's 'communicator', Marty and his team took only 90 days to create a working cell phone – brick-like in its shape by comparison with our slim line versions. It didn't have to be fancy. It just needed to do the job. This it did in theatrical fashion when Marty used a press conference showcasing the new technology to

---

[53] https://www.destination-innovation.com/how-startrek-inspired-an-innovation-your-cell-phone/

cheekily call Joel Engel, the then Head of R&D at AT&T to tell them they were far behind.

 Star Trek inspired many other technologies. I list them as inspiration to use the fanciful:

- Uhuru's Bluetooth headset.
- Portable memory – which we know as USB devices.
- Voice interface computers – Hello *Alexa and Siri*.
- Biometric data tracking for health and identity.
- GPS.
- Automatically sliding doors[54] – and even a more intelligent variety like that of Star Trek that doesn't open when someone passes by, and that opens in time according to the speed at which you approach it[i].
- The real time translator ( Skype – 2014).[55]
- The tricorder that Captain Kirk always wore over his shoulder to analyse a new planet for oxygen levels and potential diseases (now used as  LOCAD by NASA to evaluate unwanted microorganisms on the International Space Station- AND in Harvard Medical School as hand-held devices to inspect the body non-invasively – AND also by Loughborough University and the University of Leicester in England and the University of Washington.[56]
- VISOR -Geordi's eyewear that allowed him vision although he was blind. Bionic eyes were being

---

[54]Intelligent sliding doors
https://spectrum.ieee.org/automaton/robotics/industrial-robots/automatic-sliding-doors-get-star-trek-intelligence
[55] https://www.theguardian.com/technology/2014/dec/16/microsofts-star-trek-skype-translator-turns-english-into-spanish
[56] https://www.washington.edu/news/2007/08/30/star-trek-medical-device-uses-ultrasound-to-seal-punctured-lungs/

tested in 2009[57]. In 2012 the company Second Sight was formed and in that year its retinal prosthesis was approved for commercial use in Europe, and by the FDA the following year.

   and in the 4th series:
- Scotty's trade of transparent aluminium (*aluminum* in the film) for sheets of Plexiglas to bring George & Gracie, the two humpback whales, back to earth to their right time: ALON [58]now exists and is lighter and stronger than bulletproof glass.

The case of GPS and how it came to the public domain is illustrative of an early case of *we are all in this together.*

In the entertaining and prescient book 'Trekonomics[59]' in which the author, Manu Sadia, examines the economics of the Star Trek world, he records how it came to be that we can now use GPS. It was the 1983 shooting down of Korean Airline 007 with loss of all 269 people aboard that proved to be the catalyst for releasing the US Navy's satellite- based navigation system for public use.

Accident investigation had showed that due to a minor error in autopilot settings,  KAL 007 was unaware of its location because it could not effectively track where it was, and its subsequently variance of 180 nautical miles off-

---

[57] https://entertainment.howstuffworks.com/10-star-trek-technologies7.htm

[58] https://www.forbes.com/sites/sujatakundu/2015/08/19/the-engineering-of-star-trek-transparent-aluminum-in-the-21st-century/#6b0a52d7c355

[59] Trekonmomics, Manu Sadia – My copy printed in 2016

course led it into Russian airspace just prior to a missile launch test.

So that such inability to locate oneself could never again result in such a tragedy, Ronald Reagan ordered the public release of the previously proprietary Navy positioning software 'Navstar GPS' - what we today just call GPS. As Sadia points out – this is the first example globally of any major utility service being made open source – and I believe the last to date – but hopefully not the last ever.

You don't have to be a Trekkie to find inspiration as you look to a radically changed marketplace that will require totally new ways of:

- interfacing in diverse situations and for various specific reasons
- entertaining  - at home and in venues
- enjoying an immersive as well as a real life(but safe) travel experience
- shopping with some sense of tactile and true colour perception ability and interaction with the salespeople,
- enjoying sport in a stadium as a shared collective fan  experience
- creating a real audience experience for athletes and performers of all sort
- team training
- mobile medical diagnostics.

In 'The End of Big[60]' author Nicco Mele suggests a toolkit:

*Define the problem, provide a lot of data,*
*have a clear process to drive people through, and*
*make sure you have a diverse network.*

Our changing world will have far more adaptive experiences required - and your company is placed to supply effective solutions to some of them - solutions better found when you **Swivel** to change your perception.

In American Business and the Quick Fix[61], Michael McGill rails against the whole 'quick fix for management' industry: and it is an industry.  He points out that research by Cornell University and others has demonstrated that MBAs are ill-suited for small, creative, innovative, and fast growing companies. They are designed for big companies and don't offer the insight in at least one critical thing: people.

This is a major flaw.  McGill points out that results come from personal relationships, not from computer analysis.

Although analysis might offer some revealing pointers, until the data is considered by a person, it is still data. It may be plotted attractively (and in ways that can mislead you – whether intentionally or not) -but until it is

---

[60] The End of Big , Nicco Mele  - My copy printed in 2013
[61] American Business and the Quick Fix, Michael E. McGill – My copy printed in 1988

'considered' it doesn't become information. McGill points out that managers don't need an MBA, but they do need to learn.

The first step is to set aside the latest management myths and fads and to accept that the types of problems of today cannot be fixed by any one person. They need diverse input in examining their nature and developing courageously creative new ways of working forward to success.

In 'Reality Is Not What It Seems[62]', Carlo Rovelli makes an important and compelling point about where innovation comes from.

It is not from new data. It is from connecting existing known data in new and creative ways. He illustrates this by writing:

What new data was available to Copernicus?
*None. He had the same data as Ptolomy.*

What new data did Newton have?
*Almost none. Used Kepler's laws and Galileo's results.*

What new data did Einstein have to discover general relativity?
*None. He built on special relativity and Newton's theory.*

---

[62] Reality Is Not What It Seems, Carlo Rovelli – My copy printed in 2017

Rovelli summarises what these and others who create significant new insights do to achieve their innovative outputs - they build on pre-existing theories and synethize knowledge across vast fields of nature to connect them in new and unusual ways.

*Things are only impossible until they're not.*

Captain Jean-Luc Picard – Star Trek

# CHAPTER FIVE
# The sum of the parts

*Wisdom is more about perspective
than about detail.*

Edward de Bono

## REFOCUS
### *Hidden product & service assets and how and where to find them*

You have by now made a fast and pretty accurate assessment of what is fit for purpose and whose purpose remains important and has not been diminished or enhanced; what needs replacing; what is a wobble point; and what is an opportunity.

We are now going to do go on a treasure hunt and yes – look behind the sofa and in the seat pockets of the car – everywhere there may be a potential asset.

We are seeking assets we haven't recognised as such. The things and the ways of doing things that can define our ability to enhance the way we do business in a globally shifting world. These can give us a quick and 'sticky' advantage in responding to the new (and evolving) needs of our existing customers – and of identifying how some of the products and processes we consider to be 'pedestrian' (boring even) can open up new markets for a different customer group.

As Peter Drucker writes in 'Managing in Turbulent Times'[63], you should ask yourself what you are prepared to abandon so you can take up any new opportunity. He also wisely suggests you *should starve the problems and feed the opportunities.*

We have worked with companies to find new revenue streams from existing products and services, so can offer some tips. As you **Swivel**, the questions to ask are:
- What new products/services can use our old ways of making/doing things?
- What products/services can be done in new ways – and what benefit would that bring?
- What would happen if we took what we did and changed it in some way – by associating it with something else or slightly modifying it to adapt to a different need?
- Is there a bit of what we do or a component we use – that could be another product in itself?
- Is the function our products/services offer needed in another industry sector?
- If we turned it upside down what would it look like/remind us of/ - and how does that affect how we think of it?
- If it is for inside use can it be made for outside use? If it was, who would that help, and how?
- Does something we make that has serious use also have the capacity to be just fun in itself? (Think Slinky)

---

[63] Managing in Turbulent Times', Peter Drucker - My copy printed in 1980

In 'The Mind of the Strategist[64]: The Art of Japanese Business' , Kenichi Ohmae discusses market segmentation. He points out the importance of understanding both customer wants and market coverage of available services. Ohmae's suggestions of what you should note as you **Swivel** include:

### Current value perceptions

Never more relevant in a world where political relationships may be having impact on your business.

As a test of what I mean, with your team examine your current belief of the market priority on the following previously held main 'attractors' for a product or service: glamour, luxury, stroking of ego, expectations of performance because of the quality of a brand's perceived reliability, comfort, resale value, availability of spare parts, ease of purchase, and ways to communicate.

### What advantages can you exploit?

Do you have strengths in the way that you have organised your business?

Do you have exceptional customer loyalty - trust - collaborative relationships - shared commitments to values?

### What does today look like?

Surreal might be the answer, but it doesn't help define what it looks like for your client.

---

[64] The Mind of the Strategist, Kenichi Ohmae - My copy printed in 1982

Get together all who deal with clients and all who produce what you supply and imagine what your clients are feeling right now.

In an ideal world add some clients to the discussion.

What unique things can you offer that will help. This should be qualified by actually getting out there and asking if these ideas are valid. They may spark new opportunities when you engage with your clients and service providers.

Next, list all the changed aspects of the current environment as we understand it today – and some of the options of how that may change or need to be adapted. All things to consider as you **Swivel**.

### The candidates in the beauty contest

As you swivel,  it is important is to identify the products/services that are in scope – usually those that are underperforming or are no longer relevant for their original market. Then comes the challenging part: What to do in response to what you find?

Here are some examples and ideas.

### Microscope to telescope

*Many companies have a hidden asset in plain sight.*
*The problem when they are identified,*
*is whether management is prepared to take their eyes*
*from the microscope to move them to a telescope.*

# SWIVEL

We have consulted with several companies who never failed to amaze us at their ability to be totally obsessed with sales to an organisation whose core business excited them – when the product had global application in sectors that didn't – so they declined the opportunities these presented.

The 'but-I-am-rubbing- shoulders-with-fame' moments of their relatively minuscule current market was worth more to the leaders of these companies than the ability to remain in business over the long-term by any planning or global assessment of wider value.

In such cases we respectfully exit stage left, with minimal adieux.

*The penalties for myopic thinking and blinding affection for your current market proposition are high.*

In 'Scale[65]: The universal laws of life and death in organisms, cities and companies', Geoffrey West reports that historically, half of all US publicly traded companies have disappeared within 10 years of entering the market.

Gary Zook endorses this in 'Unstoppable', reporting that 153 of the 1994 top 500 US companies followed the same fate. Of the 137 who did survive, almost 6 out of 10 were candidates to lose their identity in merger or acquisition: only half were able to refocus and survive.

Such is the importance of a **Swivel** in times of crisis.

---

[65] Scale: The universal laws of life and death in organisms, cities and companies, Geoffrey West – My copy printed in 2017

A 2018 report by the Innovation Consultancy Innosight[66]tracks the remarkable shift of some USA companies from their long inclusion on the S&P Index - highlighting significant changes in what were once stable performers. In some way their market proposition no longer held the same perceived worth to consumers.

Permanence and dominance are fleeting market realities in modern times.

In light of the different organisation of life required in this rapidly changing world, it is interesting that many of the incoming 'stars' of this shift are built on platforms that suddenly may have almost no meaning unless the combination of effective restructuring and a complete change in the trust relationship can be easily resolved.

Many of the services provided by these short term stars take place in an unregulated environment: Uber – where you ride in someone else's car; Airbnb where you stay in someone else's house or apartment; WeWork and Regus – in shared office space.

Bearing in mind the Innosight report publication date of 2018, recommendations they made then for harnessing disruptive change are still worthy of consideration as you look for your hidden assets.

---

[66] https://www.innosight.com/wp-content/uploads/2017/11/Innosight-Corporate-Longevity-2018.pdf

They are summarised here:

- Spend time at the edges to spot early signs of unmet need (***Swivel***).
- Note changes in customer behaviour. What are they not buying – or what parts of service/add-ons are they not taking up – and why?
- Create a 'future-back' strategy that doesn't base itself on outdated assumptions.
- Transform at two levels – so the business core is more responsive and robust and so that effective infrastructure delivers new products/services for future needs.
- Don't change anything unless you are sure your existing structures and methods can carry you onwards as you make any transformation needed.

  *Doing nothing has costs of its own*
  *– and they are higher than those of changing.*

### Bits and pieces

As Chris Anderson pointed out in The Long Tail, 'onesies' and 'twosies' might sell in small numbers – but aggregate them and they can be worthwhile business.

As Taleb says in 'Fooled by Randomness', the frequency of the profit is irrelevant. It is the magnitude of the outcome that counts.

This is echoed in 'Unscripted[67]' by MJ DeMarco. The book is a call to make the life you wish by following your own terms – those that you may define. There are some recommended underpinnings when you do, and one of the

---

[67] Unscripted, MJ DeMarco – My copy printed in 2017

early points the author makes is that *'recurrent revenues are much more important than one time sales'*.

Don't discard the small inventory or service items that make just a bit of profit.  If you were to add up all those bits, they may surprise you with the aggregate number over a relatively short period of time.

'Moving your bits' is enabled by the ability to sell online and you would be amazed at the specialist niche groups looking for the things you may otherwise have discarded.

As Anderson say, the internet has given each of us the chance to be a mini connoisseur and there is abundance of quirky, unusual, out-of-date but loved things with a very specific function online from which to choose. Anderson gives two vital pieces of advice in selling our bits and pieces:
> *Make everything available. Help me find it.*

### Hybrids and cross-breeds – new products from old

This category of hidden assets may be the easiest. It falls into what the English call a 'blinding flash of the obvious' once you spot something that has uses other than those you are promoting.

In 'Unstoppable', Gary Zook reminds us that the incoming head of Arm & Hammer looked at that familiar little yellow box of baking soda (bicarbonate of soda) with the red logo and thought something along the lines of "I wonder how many products are in there?"

*I just checked and in 2025 according to the GreenerDeal website[68] there are at least 51.*

Just to demonstrate the expandability of alternative uses for a product – it was 43 when I wrote the first edition of SWIVEL.

The ease of reformulating and packaging baking soda may not be equivalent to the efforts you may have to employ to re-purpose some of your products or services, but when you identify them and act quickly and well, your efforts can have rewards far more enriching and sustainable than those that came from the original use.

Another example from Yamaha:  Like many products, quality pianos seemed to have met the need of the times – and then times moved on. Pianos stood un-played in many houses. However, with a modification costing $2,500 you could have your piano retrofitted so that a great artist could play to you at home. Someone can record a favourite piece for you, played by a local talented artist and send it over the phone to your piano.

Now people wanted their retrofitted piano to be tuned to performance level – so employees no longer needed to make pianos were retrained as piano tuners.

In 2023 the global piano tuning market was estimated to be USD 1.4billion annually.

---

[68] https://greenerideal.com/guides/0321-51-household-uses-of-baking-soda/

Growth to 2031 is projected to be USD 2.6billion with a compounded growth rate of 6.5%.at 5.41%.

Similarly, a piano could find little place in smaller new mass housing where busy people had little spare time to devote to their playing. But the attraction of fine performances remained – so since the constraints seemed to be threefold:

- time to learn to play at performance level
- room for a concert quality piano – and
- the burgeoning need for budding performers to have portability without compromising the quality of sound

so emerged the electronic keyboard - along with easy-to-follow instructions and excellent sound quality – a direct perceived benefit for people who measure the sound quality of the car radio before deciding upon a new car purchase.

Similarly, when the sale of microwave ovens dropped off, there seemed to be no answer to be found in attitude to the process of microwaving food – until the answer came from photographing 200 kitchens.

There was stuff everywhere. The top of the fridge was stacked with things – there was hardly any work surfaces available, and certainly nowhere for a microwave oven – or any other new appliance.

Enter an integrated microwave built into the main oven unit.

### *Functionalities - What goes where - and why*
Functionality is different from function.

A bridge has certain **functionalities** that enable
the **function** :
enabling vehicles and pedestrians to cross a gap.

The elements of functionality are often so taken for
granted that they have usually never been re-examined
since they were first designed.

Break things down and work out what are the
functionalities that allow things to perform the functions
they do – and who else needs or can use those functions?

The same functionality can have a common need within
different sectors - for equipment, for processes, for ways of
viewing things, or performing things.

It is unfortunate that we seldom look beyond the needs
of the sector with which we are familiar in order to see
those common needs and cross-supply or co-innovate. As
we have seen – a crisis of some magnitude speeds that up –
but you can make your own initiatives.

Consider this well-tuned response to cross-sector
supply – and it is all in one company. We return to Yamaha.

In the course of being fortunate enough to attend a
Yamaha new product demonstration and launch at the UK
HQ, I commented on the seeming dichotomy of a maker of
musical instruments and associated sound equipment also

being a world class motorcycle engine manufacturer. I was quickly told that it wasn't a dichotomy at all[69].

Pianos and motorcycle engines both have a core functional need - and it can be best described as 'good vibrations'.

A modern piano has a frame of cast metal that supports the enormous tension of its strings. Surprisingly, that can be between 16 to 20 tons of pressure. This frame must also be elastic enough to transmit the vibrations of those strings. This means that the frame has two opposite qualities: hard on the outside and soft on the inside.

The cylinders of a motorcycle engine have to withstand the extreme heat of the pistons and yet be adaptable to the deformation of high temperature gasoline combustion.

These are the same functionality requirements as a piano frame. No dichotomy indeed, but unless you examine the core functional needs – not obvious.

### Identifying if your gizmo fits the goozywinder

In the case of finding new uses for something you already make or service you supply, you need to be able to describe its use in terms of a new market.

Before you can do that you need to be like the judges at the Olympics Equestrian Show Jumping and not those of Eurovision.

---

[69] https://hub.yamaha.com/what-do-piano-frames-and-motorcycle-engines-have-in-common/

You need to define precisely on what you will score your product's performance – or potential performance.

Show jumping scores are based on precise timed accomplishment over a tricky course. Both timing and accuracy bear on the match of horse and rider to clearing all the jumps faultlessly within the shortest time – and with grace.

Eurovision judging has been the subject of criticism for decades and its attempts to reform using part crowd 'phone-in' judging are deemed to achieve anything but an equal opportunity  performance stage, as was clearly summarised in an article by Amit Katwala in WIRED[70] on May 18, 2019 .

The short version is that the original format of Eurovision voting favoured politically biased decisions – and the current format can be easily skewed by a 'phone in' audience voting on who they think might win –or because they fancy the lead singer – rather than on the quality of the song and the performance.

Remembering that you are in the matchmaking business – you need to describe to the potential suitor the value of the shapeliness, the relevance of the colour, the refinement of the movement, the capacity to respond not just to the suitor's needs  - but also desires.

---

[70] https://www.wired.co.uk/article/eurovision-app-voting-uk-and-bias

## *Your assessment needs to identify:*

- If you have the right sized horse to clear the jumps, with the right skill, and the right supporting team and training, and
- whether your practice of performance against expected obstacles has shown that the chances of success against stiff competition is going to be worth the considerable investment in competing.

It would seem simple to be able to break something into its component parts and identify and describe their functionalities, but in no case have we found it so. Part of the problem is how we are restricted by language in describing functionality.

You need to be able to search the web for likely matches who want the same elements – and that causes problems in description.

How do you describe speed – or weight - in terms of relevance to outcome? Fraunhofer Stuttgart has worked hard on this and has a useful thesaurus. Contact me if that has relevance for you.

We find a relaxed and informal fun approach shortens the definition time in matchmaking.

If you are developing a new something from components of something else, think in terms of minimal viable product, maximum testing. A non-functioning new product is not what you need.

And don't test in complex, high stake domains where something like a person's life and health are at stake, unlike IBM with their early efforts in medical interventions for oncology using their AI-based Watson.

The case study of the $4 billion failure of Watson for Oncology was summarised in a paper by Henrico Dolfing[71] in 2024. It offers some insight into the challenges of depending upon AI in certain domains.

IBM started with ambitious goals in 2011. After contract cancellations of key clients in 2018, Watson Health was sold in 2021.

As Watson's main diet was the practices and data used by 'Memorial Sloan Kettering Cancer Center' (MSKCC), it proved that much of what was input didn't align with real world practices. Some of its learning was on hypothetical examples. The results were considered at worst flawed, and at best simplistic.

The AI failed to cope with variations in global health systems, resource availability (different availability of medications in many countries from those of the US), and cultural practices.  There were other contributions to project failure that will all sound familiar:

- Over-reliance on a limited amount of AI training data,
- Poor messaging 'out there',

---

[71] https://www.henricodolfing.com/2024/12/case-study-ibm-watson-for-oncology-failure.html

- Inadequate collaboration with key stakeholders,
- A US-centric approach ill-suited to other cultures,
- and what many considered to have been cavalier ethics.

What is even more worrying is that these errors that were cited may persist and become part of the research lexicon for their field. In 'The Half Life of Facts[72]', Samuel Arbesman cites many serious cases of false 'facts' being cited as genuine: Things such as spinach and Popeye.

Supposedly Popeye eats spinach because it is rich in iron. In an article in the British Medical Journal in 1981 Terry Hamblin detailed how that came about. It resulted from a typo that assigned spinach a complement of 35 milligrams of iron, when it actually should have been 3.5 milligrams, as in the original research. German scientists tried to get the spinach portions correctly assigned with no success.

The myth sustains. In fact, the error gets compounded. Mike Sutton, a reader in criminology at Nottingham Trent University carefully evaluated the literature to discover that Popeye actually ate spinach because it was rich in Vitamin A.

One cannot help but wonder what Popeye and Spinach have to do with the study of criminal behaviour, but let's just let that pass.

Simple errors like this pass into the common parlance. Some have also happily been passed on to the large-

---

[72] The Half Life of Facts, Samuel Arbesman – My copy printed in 2013

language learning models of AI to be repeated extensively into the future. Actually AI corrected me about Popeye ,so it has caught up with diet facts of cartoon characters.

More dangerous are the errors where a misplaced decimal point causes an output of a figure relied upon in critical decision-making.

So while AI can be useful – the caveat is to always verify stated research or 'facts' that are offered so you are not part of the repetition of erroneous information brigade – but more importantly, so you don't factor in incorrect information  as you Swivel.

With these cautions in mind, be aware of any regulatory requirements for a future product – check the approvals process as it is now – not what it was –and then think again if your activities are best placed there, or in other aspects of refining, minimising, or expanding aspects of your current business.

### *Dress for Success*

You may have some perfectly suitable, serviceable and solid products and services that just need a new spring outfit or cocktail dress to bring them to the attention of their suitors. Take the example of Jell-O (jelly to other English speakers and to others – a gelatine-based dessert)

Most North American households in the 1950s had different shaped 'jelly molds'. The bible of the American Kitchen, 'The Joy of Cooking', had 69 recipes that used these to create jellied salads of various varieties and other sweeter jellified delights.

With the movement from the kitchen to the floors of business, American women no longer found the arrangement of tiny pieces of goodies into jelly a rewarding pastime, and the 'jelly mold' seemed to have passed into history.

After the decline of Jell-O sales throughout the 1960s, they were revitalised by the introduction of a new party dress: Jell-O Jigglers were Jell-O dressed up as Pac-Man, Batman, characters from Star Wars; Huey, Dewey, and Louie Disney ducks –and became the belle of the ball again.

A sign of the times – the next party dress was more a slinky little cocktail dress – as 'Jell-O shots' came into style with the addition of vodka or rum.

Would moving any of your products or services from overalls to opera coat, or hard hat to racing helmet, give new life and a wider or more exclusive market?

## Accidental successes
Look under the sofa – are there any accidents of invention or process that have been discarded because they didn't do the job for which they were originally designed?

Many failed solutions proved to be more useful than for the thing intended.

- Craig's List was a side project designed to connect friends in San Francisco.

- Viagra was originally designed for cardiovascular treatment.
- The microwave oven was invented when Raytheon engineer Percy Spencer was fiddling with a microwave antenna and a chocolate bar in his pants pocket melted.
- Polyoxybenzylmethylenglycolanhydride - known to most of us as Bakelite - was an accidental substitute for shellac when chemist Leo Hendrik Baekeland changed thinking from *coating* the wood to *impregnating* the wood.
- George de Mestral's dog helped invent Velcro when both it and George's socks needed de-burring.
- Patsy Sherman was trying to make a rubber material undamaged when exposed to aviation fuel when she dropped some fluid on her shoe – and that spot remaining clean when the rest of her shoes got grubby - now we have Scotchguard.

### Same product, same use, unexpected new market

Your new revenue streams may be an accident of fate. As pointed out in 'American Business and the Quick Fix', the emergence of AIDS revived the condom industry.

If one of your products or services has seen a sudden boost then all you may need to do is amplify its success by judicious promotion – or by repackaging and refining.

### Take it to the gym

Sometimes you and your team can just *Swivel* by changing the environment where your product or services sit. Put them into the context of a gym.

What would happen if your product was lighter, less costly, more robust, looked the part better, could carry more weight, went round and round and stayed in the same place, was put to music, had a stronger rack for the weights, made exercising more pleasant, could measure weight accurately, gave better encouragement, offered a better diet?

When you take your products/services to the gym – is it a modern gym, or like the last one you attended – when you were fitter and were part of the local basketball team?

Get everyone in your team to define the elements of a gym and write those on a central 'whiteboard' or someone's equivalent in a virtual world, so you have a new hybrid gym to take your products to.

Part of the skill of the **Swivel** is to imagine a new environment for familiar things. A trip the gym is always a good place to start.

### With a knob on the side it could...

Many products have undergone swift slight adjustments in the design, their chemical makeup, their order of assembly, or in some other way have responded a new need. Some of them are what a recent issue of Time[73] called a *'production shift to relevance'*.

These Covid examples give us inspiration. Radical shifts in production can be done – and fast.

———————————————

[73] https://time.com/5814509/coronavirus-marketing/

- Scottish 'BrewDog' donated 500 bottles of sanitising liquid to an Aberdeen ambulance crew in one load and more to the Royal Aberdeen Infirmary Intensive Care Unit. *Their production turnaround took just 4 days.*
- The Louis Vitton owner group LVMH did the same thing in switching from making expensive perfumes to hand sanitisers, as did Nivea, Coty, Clarins and L'Oréal ; Brooks Brothers, Armani , Nike, Prada and others in making PPE suits; a Dallas based furniture company making face masks; a northeast Texas company *using wrapping for its chocolates to make face shields*; another Texas company AK Wet Works[74] *adapting its industrial coatings equipment to develop a vapour surface disinfectant applicator able to disinfect up to 20,000 square feet an hour (just over 1,858 square metres).*
- UK based Dyson changed from making machines that suck (vacuum cleaners) to machines that blow (ventilators)
- The Royal Mint of the UK switched from making coins to making face masks – from not having ever done so, to making one every 10 seconds. Having been set the task,  the Royal Mint engineers *developed the design and mass production methods in 48 hours.*
- Italy's Isinnova that usually makes 3D printed earthquake sensor components and everyday items, switched to making valves for ventilators.

Every country has its examples.

---

[74]
https://www.houstonpublicmedia.org/articles/news/texas/2020/04/02/365693/heres-how-texas-companies-are-repurposing-their-operations-to-help-fight-coronavirus/

What are the products you already have that can be re-purposed ?

What equipment do you have that can be responsive to a future world which may be characterised by rapid shifts in regulations and impacts of damaged political relationships?

Ultimately, the critical benchmark is what value does the new product bring? As DeMarco says in 'Unscripted' :

*without value you are sailing without a mast.*

What thinking, what services, and what fun can your company generate for the new environment in which we will be living?

With a knob on the side – what could you make into something else to make life easier, more enjoyable, safer, or more collaborative?

**The risks of repurposing**
When a company provides products and services outside its original product or service line – or to a vastly different type of client, there may be insurance or regulatory issues that are better dealt with at the outset rather than should an incident occur. Someone should have the task of checking regulatory requirements, certifications, and the liabilities of working with new regulatory restrictions.

## The need for speed

Richard Florida points out in 'The Big Reset' that every recovery from crisis to date has been *spurred on by new infrastructure that can speed movement of goods, people, and ideas.*

What part can your company play in that 'speeding up' of transfer?

Does speed have a value?

Ask FedEx. Before it 'absolutely, positively had to be there overnight' – it seldom was – but now it must be.

Michael J. Kami pointed out in his book 'Trigger Points', my version printed in 1988, that:

> *Business decisions today must be made three times as fast as in the past, but with additional risk.*
>
> *You can achieve that if pertinent data are available twice as fast, communicated twice as fast, and analyzed three times as fast.*

If that was relevant in 1988, it has been accelerated even more by our current global realities.

This is challenging with things like new tariff regulations that are intertwined and are difficult to unravel in their many layers of applicability.

In a different way, speed can be defined as the one-stop ease offered by companies who recognise the challenges of the people using the equipment they supply.

A really compelling example was presented in the London Innovation Road Show of Software AG. At this there was a brilliant – show stopping in fact – presentation by Danielle Hernandez of the market intelligence firm IDC[75]. She was making the point about the urgency to reconsider the digital transformation of your company.

In that presentation Danielle explained that:

*to transform with 30 lineal steps you would travel 30 metres –but in 30 **exponential** steps you could travel approximately 25 times around the globe.*

You will see what is meant by using such an analogy by the example Danielle used.

A surgical instrument maker rethought their business in terms of the challenges I mention above. They did this in the context of recognizing the 'need for speed' with no loss in effectiveness, because lives are at stake.

From their **Swivel** the company made the decision to no longer sell surgical instruments – and they are market leaders.

Instead, the company has restructured to supply the complete surgical kit required for specific types of surgical intervention and supply it in time for the surgery.

---

[75] https://www.idc.com/

This kit comprises their products and those of other required throughout that specific type of surgery.

The kit needs to be able to be:
- delivered on time,
- to full regulatory compliance of each component part,
- with all the required regulatory paperwork completed,
- and the parts of the process that can only be completed by the surgical team to be simplified and clearly laid out,
- and then to collect the used package and components parts to be disposed of, or recycled, appropriately.

This is a lease business model.

You can imagine how it made immediate sense to the medical establishments who had previously bought and warehoused surgical instruments, then had to have these packaged with all the other required surgical material, without oversight causing any gaps in supply of even a tiny component, and get it to the right place at the right time – and to the dismay of the surgeon, the warehoused product may have long-since been superseded by an improved more modern version.

This new lease model of business was no mean undertaking. Think of the collaboration required, the cross IT platform integration, the joint level of commitment, etc.

Is it going to be worthwhile exiting the original business? In this case, I think we can all answer that in the affirmative.

Just think of all the impacts this has. It eliminates hospital ordering, warehousing, inventory control to ensure there is a complete supply of everything on the day, regulatory paperwork, and correct disposal – and makes sure the instruments supplied are the latest and not just what was bought some years ago. It is brilliant.

It is also a case of collaborating effectively with everyone in that chain.

This means rethinking the whole digital platform, allowing access to critical information by all partners supplying, including – and especially- the fulfillment partners who get the package where it needs to be in the condition it needs to be in, when it is needed – not before and definitely not afterwards.

It also means extreme due diligence in quality assurance of third-party partners.

*This is speed translated into benefit.*

It is a demonstration of exponential thinking. 'Products as a Service' has just had exponential acceleration.

What similar rethinking can you employ with what you sell?

Does it have to be sold or can you do things better by collaborating with everyone else supplying the same customer to the same ends of the finished outcome?

McGill quotes comments from a company called 'Empire Bolt' in Spokane, Washington. CEO Larry Stanley noted the difference in responsiveness in his supply chain. The big companies found it difficult to be able to ship in three days – yet he found no small supplier taking longer than four hours.

If you are a big company – never has the need for speed been more pronounced: refine your processes.

If your company is smaller – exploit your advantage.

**Repurposing IT applications**
Your legacy software applications may have suffered in the onslaught of unexpected demand to operate in different ways or to support heavier usage.

The problem is multi-faceted. Some of the problems include these conversations going on between your legacy systems and applications and new ones introduced to respond to new needs, or to fix problems, or support new or different groups or things:

**I know you are there but I am not talking to you because:**
- I don't speak your language.
- The guards won't let me.
- There is a wall between us.
- My feet are on the ground and your head is in the cloud(s).

**I don't even know or care that you exist because:**

- No one told me.
- I am just doing this job I was told to do and doing it well - so your point is?
- It's hot in this desert/ wet down here at the bottom of the ocean/ freezing here on the ice pack and I have protective gear but all you have is bling and bravado.
- I like my little corner of the world – they know me here.

In every company, versions of these conversations are now going on within your applications portfolio and/or will continue - because it's the nature of the IT beast to evolve. On that evolutionary path we end up with:

*Cockroaches* – that will outlast most things because they just manage to get the job of survival done, no matter what the environment.

*Tasmanian devils* – not the cartoon variety, but the real thing long considered extinct but suddenly discovered in a quiet and infrequently visited corner of their world. They were there all the time but we seldom were.

*Sloths* – perfectly evolved for slow and steady progress and the ability to be endearing to those who know them, and

*Dolphins* – that swim enticingly just beside the boat's progress, but you cannot quite tune into the signals of what they are trying to tell you.

If you have a better way of categorising your software apps and their position in your evolutionary tree, then make your own descriptions. If not, start with finding your cockroaches, Tasmanian Devils, sloths and dolphins and see if they are capable of communicating – or if they are, but shouldn't – or should, but cannot.  Using such descriptors takes away the judgement that may otherwise be associated and changes your survey from a witch-hunt to something more constructive, and fun.

The fix may not be as traumatic as a complete transformation –a Red Hat article on 'Making Old Applications New Again'[76] makes some suggestions. The link is in the footnotes, below. Of course unauthorised code modifications should be automatically blocked – but you may need to do some authorised repurposing.

If you have lost the plot on the functionality of something and want to make a comparison with another software application, there is a handy guide from the Boardingware Blog[77], link in footnotes.

In your assessment, check that all your IT is not just a method of what Tom Peters in 'The Circle of Innovation' calls *making yesterday's mistakes faster*.
As DeMarco writes in 'Unscripted': *We need to study failures.* This point is mentioned in varying forms by many of the authors mentioned in 'Swivel'.

---

[76] https://www.redhat.com/cms/managed-files/co-modernization-whitepaper-inc0460201-122016kata-v1-en.pdf
[77] https://blog.boardingware.com/features-vs-functionality/

## How valid is 'Just in Time'?

In 'Future Perfect'[78], Stan Davis cautions about making a more realistic evaluation of the value of inventory.

At that time he estimated that the five major components that make up the cost of inventory have the following % cost:

- carrying inventory (32%) (LOKAD puts this at 25% in 2013)
- transportation (23%)
- warehousing (20%)
- order processing (18%)
- administration (7%).

I include these percentages to make you think. What are yours? If 'carrying inventory' and 'order processing' and 'administration' haven't been reduced from this percentage within your business – they should have. Those percentages from Davis were written in 1966. Technology has moved on since then and there should be some notable differences, but I use them to jolt your thinking. More importantly – think of the surgical instrument manufacturer story.

Should you even be in the business you are now in? Can you provide more value by doing something different?

A September 2013 article on Supply Chain website LOKAD give a more recent measure: Add 20% to the current prime rate for borrowing money. For instance, if

---

[78] Future Perfect', Stan Davis – My copy printed in 1966

the prime rate is 10%, the carrying costs would be 10+20=30%. That is a dated and US-centric example but as a rule of thumb: A 0.25% increase in the prime rate could translate to $2.50 for every $1000 you borrow. It translates roughly in all currencies.

Do you know how you evaluate those costs in your company? ...and if you do – have another look and see if 'Just in Time' really has the cost benefit you believed it did.

According to LOKAD, inventory record inaccuracies, especially those of phantom inventory (goods that are recorded as available on-hand at a storage location in your electronic system but are not physically present), have several contributors:

- Replenishment errors
- Employee theft
- Customer shoplifting
- Improper handling of damaged goods
- Imperfect inventory audits
- Incorrect sales recording.

The solution: a physical count.

In 'The Average is Always Wrong[79]'Ian Shepherd warns us on how we are fooled by our own numbers by how they are displayed, and how we misinterpret what they are telling us. Shepherd's book educates us on the way that average data is misleading because it doesn't

---

[79] The Average is Always Wrong.  Ian Shepherd – My copy printed in 2020

capture variance in the data sets – the contexts within which the data is gathered.

Was it really your incentive program that increased sales after you isolated poor performance through analyzing averages? Or was one of your best groups having a bad month – maybe through causes external to them – and your 'improvement program success' merely reflects their performance returning to normal when that external obstacle was removed? He explains how a 'control group' can help you measure more effectively and result in data that really does give useable information.

Shepherd also cautions us about misplacing cause and effect in a chapter headed 'Umbrellas don't make it rain', where he demonstrates that correlation does not imply causality. He also points out something we often overlook in analyzing our data:

*History does not predict the future.*

It all comes down to what data you need, where it is stored, and how you can effectively understand it without the buzz words.

We find that if you use the data that is available rather than trying to re-assemble it in an off-the-shelf, 'make it fit into our preformatted system' product, you'll get the results needed. It's that Apollo 13 solution again. However, it may cause you to e-evaluate how all the necessary data is assembled. Be prepared for some variety of format and systems and then re-think what the best format of the future will be, so you don't have to excavate to sort the gold from the dross.

## Substance and Style and their power

In 'The Substance of Style[80]: How the rise of aesthetic value is remaking commerce, Culture, and Consciousness', author Virginia Postrel explains why the benefits of specialisation are worth considering.

Put simply: people are different. The book explains why aesthetics matter and how the way we respond to look and feel – even electronic versions – create demand. In thinking about customisation for your company – it can be very lucrative.

Author Clay Shirky, in 'Cognitive Surplus' pointed out that web pages don't have *quality* but *qualities*. His point is that clarity of design is good but not good enough because if you add other qualities, like *"the satisfaction of making something on your own, or learning while doing"*, the 'stickiness' value is highly enhanced.

A notable historic case illustrates all of these points. In FSTR" James Gleick points out that in an era when the fob watch was *'de rigueur'* for the stylish man, in 1904 Cartier made a wristband watch in response to the request of Brazilian aviator Alberto Santos-Dumont. Gleick notes that within two decades the word 'fob' had almost disappeared from the language.

---

[80] The Substance of Style: How the rise of aesthetic value is remaking commerce, Culture, and Consciousness, Virginia Postrel – My copy printed in 2003

# SWIVEL

The timing of this new perspective on an accepted form of gentlemanly timekeeping was followed by the opening of what would become Rolex, in London in 1905.

Founder Hans Wilsdorf had detailed knowledge of timepieces that had been honed during his employment by the then well-reputed watch firm of Cuno Koten, located in the Swiss canton of Neuchâtel. The company was located in the city of *La Chaux-de-Fonds*, the most important city in what is known as the 'Watch Valley'. Given its remarkable history, it is now a UNESCO World Heritage Site. Coincidentally, the city is also a renowned Art Nouveau centre, and the birthplace of both race driver Louis Chevrolet, co-founder of the company of the same name, and of the architect Le Corbusier.

In his job at Cuno Koten, Hans had to wind hundreds of pocket watches each day and ensure they were keeping perfect time. It was an opportunity to learn how different watchmakers approached the demands of precision time keeping.

When Hans formed a partnership with his brother- in - law to set up his company in London he staked a great deal on his belief in the future of the wrist watch or 'wristlet' as it was then called. His order with a Swiss company that had perfected a suitable movement for the wristwatch was the largest ever made to that time. This established a strong and enduring relationship with the company, Aegler: a relationship that continued until 100 years later Rolex success enabled it to buy the company.

It was, if you will excuse the pun, 'timely' that a few days before the outbreak of World War I, the Royal Observatory at Kew awarded the first ever 'A' certificate to the wristwatch – a Rolex (thanks to the *bobswatches.com*[81] website for explaining)

To gain a "Class A" Certificate from the Kew Observatory, a timepiece was subjected to 45 days of tests (compared to the Swiss standard of 15 days of testing) with a precision tolerance of a few seconds per day. Plus, it had to be tested in five different positions and at three different temperatures.

RAF pilots in WWII frequently replaced their inferior Forces Issue watches for the precision of a Rolex – but when captured had them immediately confiscated. When Hans heard of this, he offered that anyone writing to tell him of the circumstances of this would have their watch replaced free of charge, and it would be held to be claimed at the end of the war.

However, the institution of a 33% customs duty during the Allies blockade also impacted neutral countries – and resulted in Rolex moving its HQ to Switzerland – where it has remained: a lesson in blanket application of economic policy without consideration of unintended consequences. A cautionary note not heeded in this current era.

Having no children of their own, Hans and his wife donated the whole fortune of Rolex to the Rolex

---

[81] https://www.bobswatches.com/rolex-blog/resources/rolex-kew-observatory-certificate.html

Foundation[82] that now owns the company. Their commitments are interesting and include Awards for Enterprise, and a 'Mentor and Protégé Arts Initiative' that operates biennially to bring gifted young artists across a broad range of the arts to work with recognised masters. According to the Rolex website, these twin philosophies still underpin the pursuit of excellence at Rolex:

> *'Draw from traditions to drive innovation'.*
> *'Push back the limits to inspire'.*

Substance and style have enduring power.

Your company should examine its own qualities and how they can contribute to the globally shifting world. Not only is this the way to sustaining your company by finding its ability to respond to new needs and revived values, but it is the profitable route as well.

All this is best summed up by this quote by Virginia Postrel from 'The Substance of Style' (***Bold*** *is mine*).

*Good design is a renaissance attitude that combines technology, cognitive science, human need, and beauty* ***to produce something the world didn't know it was missing.***

---

[82] https://www.rolex.org/

**Great Dane or Dachshund? Scale to fit.**
In Cognitive Surplus, author Clay Shirky points out
something that is useful to remember as we evaluate our
current state of operation and our offerings and think about
changing some to suit new or changed needs.

When we alter the SCALE of something there are
several things to note and they all fall under this heading:

> *When you aggregate a lot of something,*
> *it behaves in new ways.*

In 'Small is Beautiful'[83]: a study of economics as if
people mattered', author E.F. Schumacher reminds us that
every activity has an optimal scale and that counter-
intuitively:

> *the more active and intimate the activity...*
> *the greater the number of relationships*
> *...need to be established.*

So we will be aware that we cannot just double the
recipe and expect the same perfect chocolate cake. We will
have to seriously consider the impact of scale on the change
and make sure the right supporting relationships are there.

Benoit Mandelbrot reminds us in 'The (Mis)behaviour
of markets' that great outputs do not always require great
numbers of supporting staff – citing the fact that at the
time of his writing in 1962, the whole monetary system of
the EU was supported by a research department of just 58

---

[83] Small is Beautiful::A study of economics as if people mattered', E.F.
Schumacher – My copy printed in 1978 – the 8th reprint.

employees. *(at the time of writing I checked and the latest numbers I could find were for 2024 – and at 62 are roughly the same.)* So, scaled outputs may not need more staff.

The fascinating and well-documented book 'Scale: The universal laws of life and death in organisms, cities and companies', by Geoffrey West, shows the remarkably similar ways that things work and how they share

*'surprisingly systematic regularities and similarities in their organization, structure, and dynamics'.*

The book explains how the individual resulting 'whole' of an aggregated system  – and your company is a system in these terms – is disassociated from the characteristics  of its building blocks, taking on quite distinctly different characteristics together than when alone.

Any aspect of the business you design for the new realities of the future should re-evaluate each building block and all its relationships. This minimises the chance to inadvertently build in unintended consequences.

**Your Great Dane**
*Big paws means your puppy will be a big dog.*

A report by McKinsey[84] on 15th May 2020 *(the six author collaborators are listed in the Appendix of a list of source books)* echoes much of what we have explored in

---

[84] https://www.mckinsey.com/business-functions/organization/our-insights/reimagining-the-post-pandemic-organization#

this book, but one interesting thing is how the scale of the organisation has frequently changed.

Lack of correctly skilled staff was the greatest limitation for future growth across most industry sectors. In the future you should assess the viability of hybrid work – some in the office and some from home, or your staff may force you to scale *downwards* through lack of the right skills at a time.

Do you source talent from a global market to work from a distance? Other companies may be surveying your own staff as likely candidates for recruitment – so making your company 'sticky' on the inside as well as extending a 'sticky' message to the market is the dual imperative as you go forward.

It may be that, like Zoom, your company grew as an accident of fate: having the right product or service at the right time.

On the 25th April 2020, the World Economic Forum (WEF) website posted an article[85] by EY's Andy Baldwin about the need to plan for the future of your company. In it, Baldwin quoted Zoom statistics: from 10 million users in December 2019, in March 2020 this grew exponentially to 200 million and by April 2020 was at 300 million.

Zoom is a company that had big paws. You could see that it was 'on trend' as it grew. You and your team may

---

[85] https://www.weforum.org/agenda/2020/04/how-to-plan-company-future-during-pandemic/

discover that your paws are also an indication of the same. Plan accordingly.

Few companies plan for such unexpected, exponential, and rapid growth. That is what my earlier book 'Shrapnel Free Explosive Growth' addresses with a six-week process to do just that – now that book has been updated for these fast changing times: '*More* Shrapnel Free Explosive Growth'.

When this happens and it wasn't in the plan (and it seldom is because most people don't plan for unbounded success) - you don't have time to spend on laborious strategies on how to cope with today as you structure for tomorrow - just like now in a global politically-induced crisis.

In both cases you have to use the inner expertise, knowledge and commitment of your teams to respond as needed – and identify what mustn't fall through the cracks between the planks as you all march forward. As Peter Drucker wrote in 'Innovation and Entrepreneurship':

*The unexpected success
is a challenge to management's judgement.*

Drucker describes a Swiss pharmaceutical company that is now a leading producer of veterinary medicine. In the 1950s, management of another firm decried use of antibiotics for animals as *'misuse of noble medicine'*.

However, in our successful company, senior leaders identified that the supplies to vets were bringing much larger profits than those for traditional use on humans and became a vet supplier. Remember the discussion about what your data is *actually* telling you?

So the company that produced the original formulas did not benefit from the much higher profitability of the less regulated market for animals. Drucker goes on to caution:

> *Look at balance sheets: Usually **directors focus on what isn't doing well** and **not on what is doing better than expected and asking why**.*

Drucker encourages leaders to put their most able people on the case of expanding on unexpected success ...and not just who can be spared. Similarly, he writes:

> *With the unexpected failure, don't rely on analytics – get out there and listen.*

You need an easy guide to walk you through a way to design your company to be sufficiently 'loose: tight' – identifying what few things absolutely MUST be done a certain way and setting the boundaries of individual decision making for most of the rest as you go forward.

In the same (WEF) article we have discussed, Baldwin stresses the need to use technology "to augment, not replace, people". This echoes Peter Drucker in 'The New Realities[86]'. In the context of stressing that where work is

---

[86] The New Realities, Peter Drucker - My copy inherited from my Dad and printed in 1989

done is the determinant for how it is done (pertinent to many of us now), Drucker makes two relevant points:

*Technology is not about tools but about how we work.*
*What can be taught must be taught*
*and this is the only way to learn it,*
*but what can be learned, can be learned.*

### Training for the Agility Course
In your teams, isolate which is which and expend your training/learning resources accordingly.

In this era many people will skill themselves, but do not assume they have the specific knowledge to deliver what you expect unless together you explore this issue and agree that the specific things needed to be learned were learned in a way that will deliver the outcomes you need.

### The long stretch – a dachshund is well suited to its purpose
Apparently a dachshund is half-a-dog high and a dog-and-a-half long.
- It was bred to hunt a 'dach' – German for Badger – and what does it now do?
- It has trained the market that it is already stretched so it is an ideal child's playmate as it's not likely to get any longer.
- It comes in three varieties all of which have developed loyal followings.

It may be that your company is now stretched – literally and metaphorically. The question is: what is the size and shape required to deliver your future outcomes.

I use the quote about measurement of a dachshund to caution you not to model on the other dogs in the Dog Show – but be happy that your odd shape is well-suited to what you need to do.

Examine the 'stretch' to find whether this new breed of animal needs something different in its care and feeding.

You should be cautious. A dachshund's design suits its burrowing, but that same design means that some things are really difficult to accomplish  - and when pushed to do so can cause long-term damage – like going up and down stairs.  Be analytical about similar constraints.

What are the limitations that your stretched company has revealed?
These need to be addressed before you spend resources on the future.

Your dachshund has demonstrated loyalty and versatility and deserves appropriate attention to the wrinkles its stretch has caused.

Unless you actively look for the damage, it may not reveal itself until it requires an emergency trip to the vet. Apply TLC and care – but you cannot do so until you know the problems created by this unexpected strain on original design.

### *Parlour tricks and enticements*
Whether your company is a Great Dane or a Dachshund, it has already had to learn new tricks without

even considering normal enticements of increased pay or bonuses. During Covid your people just got on and did it – whatever 'it' was that had to be done. Reference this as you discuss with your teams how the future looks, because they have demonstrated their capacities, their dedication to outcome, and their valuing of the society in which we live. It seems then, that we should include them in the structuring of the future rewards package.

Where you may have been thinking squeaky toys
– they may want something meatier.

*What counts is not necessarily the size of the dog in the fight; it's the size of the fight in the dog.*

Dwight D. Eisenhower

# CHAPTER SIX
# Musical chairs – who fits where and why

*Live Long and Prosper*

The Vulcan greeting
made famous by Mr. Spock in Star Trek

**Outcome assignment**

One of the greatest challenges you will have as you organise a business able to continually respond to, and benefit from, the challenges of globally shifting relationships and mandates, is that of working out who should sit where, and why, and for how long, and with whom else.

This is not a problem of staffing. It is a problem of arranging outcomes so they can be accomplished – and because the launch and mission of a spacecraft is one of the trickiest such assignments of outcome, we'll borrow some of their terminology.

If you want elegant solutions – and all the best ones are – you could take a leaf out of the book of Steve Jobs. In 'The Circle of Innovation', Tom Peters points out that the original Macintosh team was comprised of artists and engineers.

Jobs valued aesthetics and I recall him once saying that this was heightened by him taking calligraphy as a 'drop in' when he had dropped out of college.

The teacher of that class was a Trappist monk called Robert Palladino who had left the monastery and was teaching at Reed College.  Here, his teaching of the art of calligraphy focused on one style at a time, and he placed each style it in its historical context. Jobs was later to say that

> *...it was beautiful, historical, artistically subtle in a way that science can't capture, and I found it fascinating.*

We owe a lot to Palladino, because at the onset of the entrance of the personal computer, the Macintosh set the standard for beautiful fonts. But that is not why he is mentioned here.

It could be that his influence is why Steve Jobs said that he hires people for 'intriguing backgrounds' and 'extraordinary taste' - and these included artist, poets and historians. Jobs felt that these people had the 'magic' of having exposed themselves to the best things humans have done and then brought those things into their projects.
So, if you are interested in an elegant outcome – you should be looking to ensure that your team includes those with 'intriguing backgrounds' and some of that magic.

The real message here is that you should place everyone in your future- directed company in an 'Outcome Position' – not a job.

## Mission control: participative management

The fireball death on the 28th of January 1986 of seven people aboard the Space Shuttle Challenger became imprinted in horror in the memories of those who saw it on later TV footage and the few CNN viewers and those at the launch site who saw it live. Perhaps because this horror was so indelibly written on the memories of all, we have had so much commentary on its cause.

Irrefutably, it was not the O Ring itself that was truly at fault, although its failure caused the fireball. The root cause was the unwillingness of management to accept the answers they were given, so that they proceeded with a launch against engineering advice.

NASA management had previously reframed their question to demonstrate what answer they demanded when given the real one the first time. The second answer gave no more joy, so NASA management overrode the input of negative information but required the contractor who gave it to sign off that it was safe to launch.

### THE FOLLOWING PARAGRAPH IS IMPORTANT:

Since it was clear that the engineering view was that the O Ring did not have the capacity to fulfil its task at the temperatures that were predicted at the launch pad, the responsible engineer to sign off in Thiokol, the contracting company concerned, flatly refused.

### *His boss signed instead*.

*Live with that on your conscience for the rest of your life.*

Leading your company may not involve life and death decisions of this magnitude, but the example hasn't received so much press over the ensuing decades for nothing.

Sadly, management decisions that take the attitude of *'Don't confuse me with facts, my mind is made up"* occur every day – and they are always costly.

We are assuming this is not you, or you wouldn't be reading this book. But you are possibly in crisis management, needing to keep the ship afloat while you adapt it to a new environment that has elements of the familiar but is disturbingly rearranged from that which was the norm. You may not have even measured the depths of the impact the global shift in trust relationships has already had. Don't delay thinking about how they will. For they will.

You are in a different world than when your company was operating when global trust relationships that had remained relatively stable for decades, and global trade and other agreements were honoured.

Once you have a plan – which may be a dual plan of life boat management and exploration for new lands – it is vital that every element of your organisation is adapted to respond to the outcomes needed. The main challenges include:
- who is assigned to what,
- what skills are required for what,
- how people will get new required skills or adapt those they have, and

- how you will all manage to be fixers as well as initiators and
- how will you communicate effectively together?

In 'The Age of Discontinuity[87]:Guidelines to our changing society' Peter Drucker suggests that a new fundamental principle for a better society may be:

*By their performance shall ye know them.*

It is not a bad guideline for the whole launch plan. There is only one basis from which you must work and this is by outcome. Whatever methods you use, there is merit in working back from the outcomes and assigning responsibilities accordingly.

How simple is this?

It may be like someone I heard about who was interviewing for 'house share' tenants to help contribute to mortgage payments on her newly purchased home.

The first gate through which anyone needed to pass before being evaluated for 'fit' as a future tenant /house mate was to state their preferred tipple(favourite drink) .

If the answer was 'Gin and tonic', there was no tomorrow. That was her tipple and she didn't want ownership of gin bottles to become an issue. In assigning your responsibilities you need to have similar gates and the first one needs to be just as reality based. We use this

---

[87] The Age of Discontinuity: Guidelines to our changing society, Peter Drucker – My copy printed in 1971

example in our work. I donate it to you. We call it 'The Gin Gate': What is totally unacceptable an attribute in achieving this particular outcome?

This handy guide is an adaptation of one I developed when hiring for a fast growth company when people then also didn't have much time to ponder but needed good outcome-oriented people – and needed to make sound judgement in a hurry. It's a simple template. Change the qualities or each outcome required and it will quickly bring reality to your evaluation. The person you were about to offer a launch suit because of a great success at something recently may not prove to be the right choice for the particular outcome your post-Swivel plan needs.

As we together look at some examples of the types you need and critical elements in their makeup, make sure that for each you design a Gin Gate. In using the grid, don't add any more than five attributes: isolate essentials.

| Outcome evaluation grid | | | |
|---|---|---|---|
| OUTCOME REQUIRED (fill in the blank)..................................................... | | | |
| Relevant Ability/experience | High | Medium | Low |
| | | | |
| | | | |
| | | | |
| | | | |
| | | | |

In gaining some inspiration of things we might consider, let's stick with a shuttle mission because it is illustrative of what we are trying to do with the results of our **Swivel**.

Let's look at the outcome orientated people you will need to deliver your post Swivel plan.

## Astronauts: the ones everyone will be watching

Your 'Astronauts' are the people in the public eye performing the services you offer – and they are the products that make your offer a better one than that of the competition.

In both cases they will have undergone rigorous Quality Control and testing and be 'mission-ready'. They know what outcomes they must achieve and that they should do so with grace and effectiveness.

We are not suggesting that anyone is tried and tested for this Black Swan period of time – or for any of its hatching eggs. What we are suggesting is that the person assigned to each role should have sufficient background experience to call upon it and adapt it to the needs of their assigned outcome.

### *Astronaut People*

So, do you have the right people suiting up to be astronauts, or are they just the ones who you always put forward because they are familiar, or you thought they did a good job at something else, or they looked good on paper and you actually don't need to check capability?

Carey Smith, speaking on the Inc video of growing his company 'Big Ass Fans', told of growing his business internationally. He gave the example of doing 10 years of business overseas through agents.

In using agents, Smith suited up astronauts who weren't trained in the central training suite for astronauts. They were moderately successful. But then his own astronauts flew in. In the ensuing years after he sent people from the original office overseas to hire locals - exponential growth followed.

The difference came from the passion of those people who understood the product really well, who were steeped in the company culture, and who were vested in the results. They transmitted all these intuitively well to locally hired team members instead of expecting a locally hired enthusiastic person to be able to respond the same way without that background.

I commend the webcast replay (link below)[88]. It is a casebook on values-based business success.

For the people everyone is watching – your 'astronauts' are the embodiment of your company and must be evaluated not just for their skills to do the tasks that will deliver your outcomes, but to be suitable representatives not just of product or service, but what the company stands for.

---

[88] https://www.inc.com/gabrielle-bienasz/big-ass-fans-carey-smith-recession.html?utm_source=incthismorning

### *Astronaut Products*

The highflyers in your inventory may be pulling the wool over your eyes. In my experience working with clients I have found that a combination of the following are all elements of why the products/services seen as most profitable, often are not:

- the accounting systems and the way profits are measured,
- the way the company leaders become overly fond of a product, and
- the inability of others to see flaws in a product's construction that could be improved

In 'The Borderless World', Kenichi Ohmae makes the point that the biggest wool puller may be your accounting system.

How you account for profit can skew reality. Ohmae explains that an accounting system that 'remembers' losses product by product make it very difficult to understand the true state of profitability of any product. For example, Ohmae explains how in Toshiba the accounts per product start fresh every year: making a much more accurate assessment possible.

Remembering the lessons of 'The Long Tail', some of your 'back of the drawer' products may well prove to be the real astronauts.

After the cameras and bystanders have gone home, after the rocket burns out your product becomes just a dot on a horizon until your astronaut product dot is almost indistinguishable from the broader environment of constellations: as it continues on it long space journey it may well prove to be bringing returns that are significant in their aggregate.

Probe what those numbers are telling you about the niches that such products fill and see what else you have in the back drawer.

## Engineers: without whom nothing will fly
It's a great time for the engineers to huddle.

Can you exploit the fact that others in the engineering industry and certainly in the construction industry may be hampered by the inability of sub-contractors to survive intact?

Can you design better modular or offsite construction, make exceptionally well-informed use of the latest technologies like Building Information Modelling (BIM)?

To give examples of the sorts of benefit up-skilling to BIM use can give, take the example of London's Crossrail project. Their website is worth visiting (link below[89]).

Crossrail is the 73-mile recently completed Queen Elizabeth line, the east-west underground railway in London that is similar to the RER in Paris and the S-Bahn system in Germany-speaking countries, with trains operating at speeds of 140km/h (90mph). This line

---

[89] https://www.crossrail.co.uk/sustainability/innovation/driving-industry-standards-for-design-innovation-on-major-infrastructure-projects

connects the two major east west railway lines that terminate in London. In the course of the project Crossrail undertook the most extensive archaeological programmes in the UK. This again shows that one project is usually many.

I used to be a volunteer and guide at Chawton House, Hampshire, which belonged to famous author Jane Austen's brother, and where she used to visit to read from the library there. It is now a repository of the works of female authors. Somehow, Crossrail engineers learned that in the house is an ancient screen with a map of London showing all its underground streams. After a visit by Crossrail engineers, this knowledge was also added into the BIM model.

The map on that screen represents a meticulous survey undertaken by John Roque from 1739 to 1746, when it was published. It has much relevance to a now much-changed London and to the engineers who were set to burrow beneath it without creating upset to the over-ground fabric.

It is interesting that after using theodolite bearings from church steeples, measuring distance in the then traditional measurement of chains (*66 feet or 20.11 metres),* and cross-checking actual against calculated measurements, to ensure absolute accuracy, Roque had people physically 'walk the map'.

Whether using the engineering tools of today or in the past – such extra detail-orientated actions should also be employed by your engineers in redesigning products and operational structures.

For Crossrail, with this input, BIM enables 3D modelling to illustrate the complex interaction of utilities around stations and identifies unambiguously the maze of underground cables and pipe systems that need to be avoided during construction. It has managed through one centralized database the following:

- 25 design contracts
- 30 main works contracts
- 60 logistics main works contracts and
- has produced over 1 million CAD files to be accessible for guidance.

Given all that, one of the key Learning Points from the project was that the Change Control process wasn't helpful – there was a need for passive 'in there' communication by way of a more seamless SharePoint integration across the many contracting organisations who together delivered the project. Their website offers all their learning for free. https://learninglegacy.crossrail.co.uk/

Perhaps tools such as BIM can help you get to the front of those heading in the same direction as your company, and ensure your future missions are effective.

No matter how effective or skilled your engineers are, it is always useful to keep in mind the research of Russian engineer (and Sci-Fi writer) Genrikh Saulovich Altshuller who developed the 'Theory of Inventive Problem Solving', known more often as TRZ.  From his research on patents he came up with these conclusions:

*Problems and solutions are repeated across industries and sciences, as are patterns of technical evolution, and the patented innovations all used scientific effects from outside the field for which they were developed.*

You could summarise by saying that 'somewhere, someone has already solved the problem'.

So – look around at parallel worlds and outside your own discipline to see what can be adapted or adopted.

### Scribes: documenting and disseminating information

One of your future products could well be that of documenting your experiences of running a business effectively –with all its warts and all challenges.  With organisations and companies embarking upon something new I have always encouraged documenting of the progress – including video and photographs - because you simply cannot create those moments again and they can have real value.

When you document your new products/ services and structure – use fewer words and better analogies and images. For one thing you haven't time to create illuminated letters worthy of an ancient manuscript at the beginning of each page – and for the other you are going for 'stickability'.

Perhaps your previous documents were never fit-for-purpose anyway, but you spent money on creating them so are determined to use them. This symptom I have encountered many times when I pointed out how a particular piece of literature or an image was of appalling quality that didn't endorse the value of the brand.

By contrast but falling under the same label as 'worse than useless', I had a document presented to me that was to entice new occupants to a council-built industrial site in rural Australia. It gave not one single business case reason to become a tenant but was of beautiful quality. I asked what result it had achieved. The woeful answer? They sent out 200 and got no response so they put the rest in the cupboard under the stairs – and this was before we all knew that this is where future magicians reside.

If either example rings even faintly true to your teams, which it shouldn't because if it rang true to you it wouldn't still be in circulation because you'd have done something better, then take input and either change your scribes or give them unambiguous specification.

Then be unrelenting about the fact that the result needs to be effectively designed so it can be reasonably expected to deliver the outcome intended. In such cases there is a clue in the name of what I am suggesting: "*User* review".

## Quartermasters: keeping supplies at the right levels

If you find that because of market shifts you have supplies of things you wish you didn't have – there are two obvious remedies –and probably lots of others as well. The obvious ones are: Who else needs them? – and - What else can we make with them? /How can we use them for something else?

They may also be guideposts to the future - what ideas do they generate?

**Meteorologists: Good to go?**
This is a skill you all unconsciously honed during Covid lockdown. You were constantly evaluating the climate to judge what was happening in your area of interests – business and otherwise.

In the environment at the time of writing in 2025 this habit of horizon scanning will become even more finely honed. You need to be more iterative and steadfastly hold what we call 30/30s. These are the meetings where you re-evaluate your chosen pathways forward to test new direction. From these you can avoid making big mistakes later by making and learning from small mistakes or new pieces of information that may influence your next 30 days.

It is useful to remember that although decent weather is required for a shuttle launch it is not always required at the launch pad of business.

When new CEO Tony White came to Perkin Elmer, he questioned the plans in place to break off Applied Biosystems (AB) , a company they had purchased, and diversify its parts across the whole organisation. White did a ***Swivel*** that showed a more 360° perspective on AB.

Bear in mind that Perkin Elmer had done a previous SWIVEL in purchasing Interdata to form a Data Systems Group – later exiting that market. The remaining portfolio served automotive, medical, aerospace, and photography.

Instead of breaking up the whole, White did a SWIVEL *Again*: he created a new company that amplified the benefits that the AB instruments offered to the then current investigations of the human genome under the Life Sciences group of PE.

The new company, 'Celera' is the same one that was the first to sequence the human genome, winning ahead of even the government-funded company employing Dr. James Watson, attributed as co-discoverer of the double helix.

Celera won the title but the effectiveness of the AB instrumentation in facilitating that win made it the leader for genome analysis.

Celera has been brought back under the Perkin Elmer brand since then, under the new PE livery. Innovation continues and operates through wide collaboration under a Scientific Advisory Board and a Customer Advisory Board, to maintain the focus on real-world outcomes.

An Advisory Boards needs to be one of friendly critics and not be a chorus of praise.

### *Broadcasters*: getting the message out
To make sense of your assessment and clearly define your options and then refine them, requires effective use of languages. As John Steinbeck wrote:

*Ideas are like rabbits.*
*You get a couple and learn how to handle them,*
*and pretty soon you have a dozen.*

But to be able to describe what a bunny looks like requires the right words. Without the right words there is no way you will have an effective idea breeding program.

In 'Words in Flow', Jack Ricchiuto records from his research of award winning writers that many commented that when they want to know what they think, they write.

This is underpinned by studies in neuroscience[90]. Studies showed many interesting differences between typing and handwriting (including the cognitive advantage of handwriting with a stylus on a tablet vs. typing on a keyboard) .

Among these are the fostering of deeper thought, critical analysis, and creativity by handwriting. This seems to be due to giving the brain has more time to synthesize ideas. Studies (including those made in Japan, Norway, and the USA) show that people remember information better when it is hand-written compared with when it is typed.  In another study hand writing also gave faster recall.

So when you are planning, I stress the importance of the written word and your use of a book for each member of your team as you **ASSESS** and assemble your ideas and analyses.

---

[90] The Neuroscience Behind Writing: Handwriting vs.Typing—Who Wins the Battle? 2025

In the same book, Ricchiuto makes an important point: stories turn writing from telling to showing. This can be expanded to say that all your ideas need to be written down in any order or format – clear of otherwise – BEFORE they are refined to be expressed in concise detail by clear writing.

It is easy to gather ideas, but to crystallise the true meaning behind each one and isolate its useful essence is where language comes into it. This is where your 'So What?' question helps drill down to what that essence is - then the clarity of the language distils it.

Before you can get a good message 'out there' you need to have refined it 'in there'. We tend to be focused on what messages we need to get to the market but anything we send externally will be measured against the effectiveness of our '*Hello in there*' messages .

**Hello in there**
Some of your broadcasts are not in words. I recall the song by Ronan Keating that speaks to this. I have borrowed some of his words, for although they were written of love, they also apply to the messages you are sending:

> *Try as I may I could never explain*
> *what I hear when you don't say a thing...*
> *You say it best when you say nothing at all.*

The things you haven't said have already spoken loudly to your own people – and those people include the families of your staff. They are *all in this together*– so are more aware of those messages as the world tilts, and they probably receive them loudest of all. If you've acted in ways that show you genuinely care for your staff, then the future message you send in words will have more 'stickiness'.

Of course the contrary holds true. If you could have done better in the past– say so. Honesty about what those things were, together with their remediation, will bring your credibility forward, if not to its optimum – at least to a place where you can continue building.

For messages without words - do you use monitoring software to keep tabs on your home working team?

Writing for the website RNZ on 2nd June 2020, Emma Hatton reported that **employee monitoring software saw a 300% surge post-lockdown** in New Zealand - and no – I didn't misplace any zeros – **300%**. When that Black Swan's egg hatches it will not be pretty.

*First point:* what happened to 'Our people are our best asset?

They are? So what happened to trust? If they check out a YouTube video or just sit and think, as long as they get the job done your minute by minute monitoring is sending out very direct signals that don't need translating. They write in Neon letters a metre high (or 6 foot) and flashing: 'I don't rust you'.

*Remedy?* Stop trying to micro-manage and aim for evaluation solely on outcomes. Take that old fashioned concept that never goes out of style: trust your own people and build that also never out of style thing called RELATIONSHIPS.

The only way to dig up from that grave is to start behaving as if you mean what you say – and by the way – it's a long way to the surface from that grave you dug.

*Second point:* If you ever wonder about the dangers, see Hewlett Packard for further details. Their efforts ended up in $14.5m damages having to be paid in 2006[91][92], the complete loss of face in the market, and that message in a Neon sign standing at probably an even greater height than any of its buildings as it flashed and broadcast to the global staff: 'We don't trust you'.

The impact of this spying on employees (which is admittedly taking 'monitoring' up several notches) has written HP into the coursework for most university management courses, into books on company ethics, into case law for the legal professions -  and into commentaries on the future efforts of HP to be seen as an ethical company.

Even more damaging has been the long-lasting effect on HP staff when they who have to pass an Ethics Course. Everyone I knew who had to take the course annually made similar utterances to the effect that 'it doesn't matter how ethical we are if the people at the top behave the way they do'.

---

[91] https://www.latimes.com/archives/la-xpm-2006-dec-08-fi-hp8-story.html

[92] https://www.wsws.org/en/articles/2006/10/hepa-002.html

This is a place in history you don't need, but worse than that – it loses any goodwill you have with your own people and any message you send '*in there*' will come back to you only as an echo. You can only expect that echo to be a mirror of yours and its message is: '*We don't trust you either*'.

*Current legal guidance*: For some current legal guidance for the UK and Europe, in the footnotes is a link to Fieldfisher,a European Law Firm dealing with risk. During Covid, Olivier Proust and Sixtine Crouzet posted a useful article[93] with legal guidelines[94]. Some principles remain after the pandemic and they warn that:

*Unlike other forms of employee monitoring (such as the use of CCTV cameras), online monitoring is not so obvious for employees and can easily go unnoticed. In such circumstances, the border between lawful and covert surveillance is very thin.*

The guidance reiterates our statement about responsibility lying with you to ensure third parties comply with local and national employment law in any monitoring of employees that takes place.

On the other hand, laws in the USA are profoundly more accepting of employee monitoring and most of the following cases are actually legal:

---

[93] written by on 14th April 2020
[94] https://www.fieldfisher.com/en/services/privacy-security-and-information/privacy-security-and-information-law-blog/the-risks-of-online-employee-monitoring-during-the

- Keeping track of what is typed
- Recording Internet activity
- Taking screenshots
- Using a device's webcam
- Noting which employees access what files and when
- Monitoring an employee's physical location using GPS
- Measuring the employee's productivity, such as noting a computer's idle time or how long an app or piece of software remains open

The fact that most of this invasive control and tracking is legal in the USA reminds me of something I once told the CEO of a firm for which I worked:

'I can have any number of jobs, but I only have one set of integrity. I will not be pressured to change HR records'.

You should consider the same adherence to values and trust when rebuilding effectively to survive whatever storm approaches in this tilted world order. Outside of wartime, never have '*Hello in there*' messages been so vital as those to the population of all countries facing big a shift in world order as has been announced in early 2025.

*Trust doesn't get awarded, it has to be earned.*

Don't act like such an over-protective parent. State the facts unambiguously with confidence and clarity. Ask for involvement in developing and delivering the solution for the company.

Stand for something - and  that something should be directly drawn from your core values and the ability to **Swivel Again**, read the realities, and act like a responsible parent.

Be wary of the fact that in many companies each manager need to repeat the message of top management in words of their own – or feel the need to do so. STOP THEM. Be like Michelle the French Resistance leader in the TV comedy 'Allo. Allo'.

*Listen very carefully. I shall say this only once.*

Say it once to everyone – but then in smaller groups repeat the message personally and enter into dialogue. That dialogue is part of your Swivel – and from it may come the kernels of value from which you can build for a future in an unfamiliar landscape.

## Hello out there:
### *NASA's clarity*

NASA has a Launch Commentator whose commentary of events is what is broadcast externally from countdown to splashdown. This is a great Fail Safe to make sure that messages are given by someone seeped in the 'in-speak' that every industry sector has, well-versed in the technology and how things work- and why, and who does what - and why, and how things should happen -and why.

This makes sure that we don't have a misunderstanding similar to the way we thought about six degrees of separation. We get the *full* message with all its details clearly stated. This reduces the chance of your message being falsely summarised into a catchphrase that isn't the full story – and like Pandora's Box lets loose the rapid incorporation of a misunderstood point to be quickly accepted as being what was meant.

As Karl Albrecht notes in 'The Creative Corporation, the media environment can be described as 'Packaged Fear'. Make sure your message doesn't get re-packaged.

### *PANDORA's story*

The recounting of the myth of Pandora's Box is a classic case of just this sort of misinterpretation – and of the way words can be variously interpreted.

The back story is that when Prometheus stole fire from heaven, the King of Gods, Zeus, used Pandora to wreak his vengeance. Epimetheus was the brother of Prometheus and Zeus presented him with Pandora – who infamously opened the 'box' and let into the world evils that included sickness and death – which of course could not be put back in again. The only thing left inside was 'Hope'.

Now we come to language and the messages of Pandora's Box to those of us *'out there'*. The 'box' is apparently more correctly translated as a jar.

'Hope' can be the false hope that removes us making an effort for ourselves because we 'hope' something will come along to redeem the situation. The other 'Hope' is the all sustaining 'hope' that keeps us going against the odds – a positive force for humanity.

The academics are in constant debate over the true nature of the 'Hope' inside the box/jar. Artists continue to be interpreting Pandora in image, in poetry and in theatre – and in the kaleidoscope of interpretation that these presentations of the myth offer, we can twist them to whatever interpretation we prefer.

In this book we keep reiterating the message of General Sullivan and Colonel Harper  in their book of the same name*:*

*Hope is Not a Method'.*

Your broadcast 'out there' should avoid the any possibility of Pandora-type misinterpretation because *we hope* it will be interpreted correctly. It must be unambiguous.

### Launch Commentator

You need such a 'one voice' Launch Commentator for your newfound direction. Please be sure the message that is broadcast has passed your scrutiny and has no words or phrases that can be misinterpreted.

Any messages should be crafted without emotional overtones – if they need to be there, add them later. That keeps the base message clear.

My mother's mantra : *Short, Sharp and Shiny,* is a good benchmark'. She also had a great piece of advice – and this is about the messages sent *'out there'* inadvertently.

*Never write anything
you don't want to see in the headlines tomorrow.*

Smart woman, my mother.

Your broadcast 'out there' should avoid the any possibility of Pandora-type misinterpretation. Chris Anderson in his follow-on book 'The ^LONGER Tail[95]' offers a useful caution.

---

[95] The Longer Tail, Chris Anderson – My copy printed in 2009

Companies often say they want to hear from consumers but he suggests you embark on this carefully because in his experience, they may out-broadcast you with their *'Hello in there'* suggestions, corrections, ideas, opinions and generally exhausting efforts to communicate with you.

## Broadcast editors

'Straight and Crooked Thinking' was written by psychologist Robert Thouless and goes into a great deal of detail about the manipulation of language – intentional and unintentional. He stresses the importance of precise definition to make our messages understandable to others. In this context he warns against the use of words or terms that have indefinite or changing meanings.

When working with our clients we warn against using what I call 'bucket terms' and describe these as the sort of thing that everyone will agree with, but no one can define. 'Bucket Term' phrases are tempting but they diminish your message.

In volatile times, the messages you send out about your company can have far reaching impact – for good and for ill. Be watchful of what you communicate and how, and do so thoughtfully and with a good writer *(and if you add apostrophes where they are not needed, lots of us will be very cross)*.

When John Kotter wrote 'Our Iceberg is Melting[96]', it wasn't a children's' book: the tag line is 'Changing and Succeeding Under Any Conditions'.

This is the fable of Fred the observant penguin who saw the risk of their melting iceberg, managed to employ Alice

---

[96] Our Iceberg is Melting, John Kotter – My copy printed in 2006

from the Council of Ten, and demonstrate to 'No No' and other doubters why he believed his theory was right.

By changing perspective and using the example of a seagull exploring widely, the penguins set their strategy and formed the right teams to create the urgent change to survive by moving to another iceberg. The moral of the story?

Handle the challenge of communicating the need for change well, and you can prosper greatly.

Handle it poorly, and you put yourself and others at risk.

The power of the fable is that it creates shorthand we can use when making out *'hello in there'* messages. We can refer to 'Fred the Observant' and 'No No' with impunity because they now come with their stories attached. You may wish to create your own fables that do the same.

### The truth about six degrees of separation

In 'The Tipping Point' Malcolm Gladwell  expands on the origin of the concept of 'six degrees of separation' – that 1960s experiment by psychologist Stanley Milgram that had such remarkable results.

Milgram was exploring the dimensions of connection in a global world. He gave a chain letter to 160 residents of Omaha, Nebraska and asked them to get it in as few connections as possible to a stockbroker who lived and worked in Sharon, Massachusetts.

The originator and each subsequent 'Connector' wrote his or her name on the packet before sending it to the next. Remarkably, the letters arrived in 5 or 6 steps: hence the 6 degrees of separation. But Gladwell explains that all degrees were not equal.

*It proved that 24 letters reached their destination at Milgram's home and the rest at his office. Of those arriving at home, **16 came from the same person**, a clothier. The majority of **the balance arrived at his office via two other people**.*

Although everyone employed a different strategy, eventually **3 people were responsible for half of the results.**

It hearkens back to the example in a pharmaceutical company and the two people being responsible for the greatest successes – two people who had been totally unidentified before someone dug a little deeper in their *Swivel **Again*** to find new inventions.

As Gladwell says, six degrees of separation doesn't mean that everyone is linked to everyone else in just six steps. This is an important differentiation from the common use of the concept – or should I say misinterpretation of the real meaning behind it.

*The true meaning of six degrees of separation is that a very small number of people are linked to everyone else in a few steps,*
***and the rest of us are linked through those few.***
*(my summary in bold).*

The fact that the principle of six degrees of separation is so often misapplied – just as with the Pandora myth – is witness to something you need to be aware of when you go into the broadcasting business.

You need to be SPECIFIC about your message and what it means – not allowing people *to interpret for themselves* your true meaning.

### *Three characters critical to the success of your broadcast*

In The Tipping Point, Gladwell has three useful labels for effective broadcasters: Connectors, Mavens, and Salesmen. The other lesson from this story is that of the power of the 'Connector'. These are people with a real gift for bringing the world together. Gladwell claims to have experimented in a variety of social settings to find out if connectors are to be found in predictable palaces. The short answer is no.

Across the socio-cultural range of society there are just some people with the happy knack of getting to know a lot of people. There probably are some in your company. If there are, you will find them on your **Swivel**. They will no doubt be connected to other connectors. Your team will know some connectors and you can together work out how best to employ them in your broadcasting efforts.

In further discussing 'Connectors', Gladwell uses the example of Roger Horschow whose 'Horchow Collection' was one of the best catalogues of wonderful gifts I have ever received in my mail box (and paid to be forwarded when I moved – pre-internet). This preceded the e-commerce catalogues of today because it was the first that didn't have a retail outlet of any sort but was purely mail order. Sadly, Mr. Horchow died in 2020.

Horchow had a knack of collecting people but when Gladwell asked about how it had helped his business he seemed puzzled. He didn't collect people as a business strategy. He just liked people. I can attest to that.

I wrote to Roger Horchow when I lived in Galveston and his company (an early 'equal opportunity for all company') was based near Dallas. I think I had suggested a product for inclusion but the important point is that I got a reply from the man himself with a lengthy explanation about the prospects for said product (not mine – I am a Maven, remember?) and I was deeply impressed.

Many years later, living in Germany, I wanted to ask if Mr. Horchow  would be interested in leading a project of a client of mine. I couldn't track him down but found his daughter's location and sent an apologetic note for intruding and asking if she would be so kind as to forward. She did. Mr. Horchow again wrote back himself, this time courteously explaining that he was busy producing theatre on Broadway – a passion of his, so would not be available.

To put this reply in context, I had missed learning of his Tony Award winning productions of 'Crazy for You' in 1992 and revival of 'Kiss me Kate' in 2000 (I was in Australia). For some reason my usual internet sleuthing just couldn't find his location or contact and certainly had not alerted me to his new successes.

Ever the gentleman, he was not affronted by what proved in the circumstances to be a naïve approach.

Perhaps this is also one of the valuable qualities of a 'Connector' – it is why they can connect: they have grace and charm and dispense it with natural ease.

So let's see if you have 'Mavens' as well.

Apparently, Mavens have a wide following of people who trust their judgement, and their networks cross many social-economic groups. They are NOT persuaders. The reason Mavens give away information is that is useful and they want to educate and help. I guess I might be a considered a maven in writing this book.

Your broadcast team needs to include a Maven or two, or know some outside the company and make them part of your unpaid marketing team.

Mavens are both teachers and students and better teachers by being lifelong students – so add to their accumulation of knowledge by alerting them to the usefulness of your business offer and why that is important in this fast-moving world.

In our **Swivel** context, 'Salesmen' are people who have what I call *'The IT factor'* in my book 'The Cuban Approach: the art of letting go'. This is something that is almost impossible to describe but you know it when you see it  - and you most certainly know it when you don't.

These are not caricatures of a 'salesman' but genuinely influence the sale of things they believe in by a combination of enthusiasm, passion, charm and…well, the indescribable 'It'. Whatever 'It' is they have it in spades, and if they could bottle it, could make a fortune. As they can't –just be happy to employ them within your forward plans – whether they work for you or better, if they don't.

### *Sweepers*
In software development David Heinemeier Hansson recommends that you limit to a team of three to develop the first version of an app: a developer, a designer and a "sweeper". The "sweeper" is the roaming interface between the other two.

The same applies with your business when you Swivel.

A very small team of the right people who thrive on constraints brings out their creativity in problem-solving. Here, you need people who can park a preconception, not spout a mantra of their latest fascination with a method or technology, and who respond fast to obstacles with workable, simple solutions that are intuitively elegant. They should also be eloquent.

*By eloquent* I mean that they must be able to describe something graphically in a way that immediately captures the point – storytelling refined. To be eloquent means to be intensely well focused.

*To be elegant* means to be beautifully crafted so what is offered is intuitively clear from first introduction: it looks good, it tells what it does simply but with impact and has shed everything un-essentially. In short: streamlined and immediately pleasing when seen.

Remove the person who is a fantastic source of every piece of information available on a particular technology or methodology.

Such people are intensely valuable because they come from the University Without Walls where people teach themselves stuff out of their passion and interest.  But they are the backroom crowd: your walking knowledge vacuums. Keep them away from communicating anything to a wider audience. Concise is not in their repertoire.

This small team will communicate better and faster and their chief communication path is with the customer in a fast feedback loop that improves design iteratively. If they are in different time zones this forces communication by email or messaging.

When you have to write something in refines your thinking: it also creates a record of thinking paths.

Gladwell simplifies the definitions:

**Maven**s provide the message.
   **Connectors** spread it , and
      **Salesmen** persuade us to believe it and act upon it.

# SWIVEL

To be an effective broadcaster, you need all three types and a **Sweeper** to ease interactions.

*I figured something out.*
*The future is unpredictable.*

John Green

# CHAPTER SEVEN
# Piggy Banks and Purse Strings

*About the time we can make the ends meet,*
*somebody moves the ends.*

Herbert Hoover

## FINANCES

We are about to look at some options for your future business, so don't make financial decisions before you review them and see if they prompt other alternative.

### *Availability of cash reserves and investment*

Times like this point to the value of industry cluster groups, business associations and other support groups. They are usually excellent sign-poster groups directing you to what available assistance there is for your type of company.

A poll of small business by Harvard Business Review **indicated** that of their surveyed companies fully 30% doubted their ability to re-open following the Covid pandemic. If when you survey the results of your SWIVEL to deal with the current shift in the global marketplace this is your final conclusion too, then there is an old adage: *your first loss is your best loss.*

Don't make the decision before making a review of all alternatives but if reality proves truly devastating you may have to shrink to grow – or start again another day – or something else - but while remaining determined and optimistic, don't be unrealistic.

We are going to look at some elements you may wish to include in your short and long-term business forecast/plan. It will be wise to have updated current business accounts – and keep them updated. You are planning for recovery that will be slim in the first 2-3 months, but impact will probably sustain in a damaged economy for 2-3 years. You should then have a virtual meeting of directors with clear and accurate minutes to discuss the accounts and future plans and address any issues.

### *Financing*

Banks are usually more responsive if involved from the start but get your beans in a row so you can set out the case factually before you engage in a conversation.

Also, be careful about seemingly favourable terms that require any *quid pro quo* such as personal guarantees or apparently good terms - but harnessed to compound interest. As you prepare your case, se careful about 'creative accounting' using non-GAAP metrics.

If you wonder why, see rulings about Uber's efforts and of the more open Stripe metrics – also not allowed by the SEC. If you are not in the US, the same types of warnings apply. Shoving too many negative charges under the umbrella of the current shifting market influenced by the ups and downs of tariffs might not protect you from a downpour of official review.

*You might feel the need for a massage to relax you with all the financial pressures you face – but massaging your accounts is not the way to resolve the issues.*

If you are aware of the challenges that border control software has in dealing with estimating the tariffs due on imported goods, don't try to game the officials, knowing they are understaffed to spot your creative numeracy. Tasked with heavy control that is unable to be enacted at the current time as widely as officialdom seems to think possible, such evaluation will most probably be made in retrospect.

The critical thing is to communicate with your suppliers and your customers and find out their status and the terms they will offer.

If someone owes you for outstanding invoices, move to get these paid before undertaking any more work for them. Make sure all work already completed has been invoiced and that the invoices are error free. This is no time for rework – you want the payments as soon as you can get them, so minimise the opportunity for debate. You will need a financial cushion as impacts of imported goods or components hit you in places that you may now not suspect.

Find what is relevant to your needs once your wobble points give you valuable information about the status of business now.

**Warnings about insolvency**

Trading while insolvent has legal implications on the company directors and liability may well fall to them if not handled well. If your company seems to be in such a dilemma, get advice immediately you have all your facts.

There are several forms of insolvency:

*If you cannot pay money owed on time,* then technically your company is insolvent – but in this period of global uncertainty there might be a sliding scale depending upon your ability to respond to outstanding debts and obligations.

*Balance Sheet Insolvency* is when your assets don't cover your liabilities. 'Contingent Liabilities' may also push the company to insolvency...these are things that may occur depending on the outcome of a future event and where the cost of that liability can be reasonably estimated.

*Cash flow insolvency* is just as it sounds. The assets might be there but be not able to be realised in time to pay outstanding debt. If your company can be demonstrated to be long-term viable, you may be able to negotiate a way out of this form of insolvency.

**Cash flow reduction**

Before deciding you are insolvent, seek other financing, and where possible negotiate new terms for contracts and with landlords- all these can redress imminent and unserviceable debt.

In the latter case there are four obvious options: discounted rent; deferment (be specific or together negotiate an agreed period – perhaps with a mid-term or fixed point in time review); a rent-free period (again – agree something specific); reduction in service charges.

If you own your property, is it worth more than your business?

Whatever is proposed, do so in writing so it can be considered factually by the recipient. Whatever is agreed, have the agreement documented appropriately so there can be no opportunity later for misunderstanding.

*An investment in knowledge pays the best interest.*

Benjamin Franklin

# CHAPTER EIGHT
## Pre-flight checklist

*Life must be lived forwards,*
*but can only be understood, backwards*

Kierkegaard

### How a 360° view can save the ship from sinking
Your ***Swivel*** has given you new perspectives to
challenge what we all thought was reality. Probing more
deeply can find a lot more things than a few coins in the
creases of the sofa and a surplus of fluff. Here are some
interesting factual comparisons to illustrate this. The first
example demonstrates something about which author
Antony Jay cautions in his book: 'Management and
Machiavelli: Power and authority in business life'. He
points out that:
*understanding economics*
*doesn't need an actuary, it needs a visionary.*

### Qualifying predictions of market behaviour
Our first example comes from 'The (mis)Behaviour of
Markets[97]'. Here, Benoit Mandelbrot writes about the laws
of physics and how the dimension of a thing varies
according to the perspective of the viewer.

---

[97] The (mis)Behaviour of Markets, Benoit Mandelbrot - My copy
printed in 2008

In the book he relates the laws of physics to our misjudgement of the behaviour of markets, and in doing so discusses fractals – the replicating 'roughness' of shapes that underpin all of nature and scales up and down by a very specific amount. For our purposes, it is useful to note that he points out that fractals are not 'things' themselves – the term describes their common properties. We often make the same mistake in how we describe 'things' in our own organisation.

What we need to do is identify relevant common properties – patterns of roughness that make our company value proposition different and useful. You do this best when you **Swivel**.

Mandelbrot writes that if you sat in Wall Street your perspective may clearly show a perception of market asset allocation based on a something called the Markowitz-Sharpe Portfolio Theory- where people are expected to manage their money in the following ratios: 25%cash, 30% bonds and 45% stocks.

If you **Swivel** – or had swivelled in 2008 – an OECD study would give a new perspective based not on theory but on reported asset allocation. That swivel would educate you that this U.S. held theory is not the way people think – and it varies by country. The study showed marked differences:

Japanese household...53% cash, barely 8% shares
Europeans keep 28% cash, 13% in shares
Americans ... 13% cash and 33% stocks.

If your market is global, you need to recognise that the single common point of view may be fragmented into not one single point of truth, but into nuanced versions of what you expected. Verify all assumptions as you assess both your current state and potential opportunities.

## So what? Keep challenging

With every wobble point and every building block you find as you *Swivel*, we recommend taking on the military's helpful question as you think of every point – both plus and minus.

That question is simply: So what? This is the quick way to sort out real potential and to rapidly define real problems. Isolating the real issue or benefit is critical in using the information you find from your *Swivel*. The question 'So What?' brings you to the specifics, not the generalities.

## Map your holding pattern

The world doesn't stop going around while you *Swivel*. You must have a holding pattern that is sound enough to keep the existing business solvent and operable and the people as happy as you can make them under the circumstances – and you must be aware of all the messages you are sending – both internally and externally.

We hope you immediately put a hold on all marketing messages until they could be vetted as setting a tone appropriate for the new environment in which we live.

If not, do it now. Right now.

The wrong tone or message at this vulnerable time can have lasting and damaging effects on market perception and on your ability to keep and attract the best people to your cause. It can also expose you to market expectations you may be unable to deliver due to factors beyond your control in this interconnected global economy.

Make an interim plan. Let everyone know it's an interim plan. The plus side is that everyone will have more tolerance for delays in new direction, in change in itself, than you have ever had before – as long as you keep true to your values and treat everyone fairly.

**Step this way - Order of priorities**
**The British Army Household cavalry 'stable' priorities**

The British Army Household Cavalry are the most senior regiment in the Army. They have the duty of protecting the sovereign and you will probably know them from globally televised pageantry of ceremonial occasions involving the royal family. The Household Cavalry has a small sign on the side of the stables on Horse Guards Parade. It says simply:

> Horses first
> Men next
> Officers last

You may not have horses, but you have to set similar simple priorities.

## Heathrow Airport priority measurement
Some years ago this was Heathrow's summary of their business plan. Yours should be as simple
Are people safe?
Is the place clean and tidy?
Are people happy?

### *Fire! - or - 'We have an empty fire extinguisher'- Urgent / Important?*
In the course of ordering your priorities, you will have to make critical decision about whether a thing is urgent or important, because that affects where it sits in your list. This matrix that follows may be familiar with you but it is useful prompt.

| | | Urgent | | Non-Urgent | |
|---|---|---|---|---|---|
| **Do it Now** | Important | Crying Baby Kitchen Fire Some Calls | Exercise Vocational Planning | Schedule, Do ASAP |
| Delegate or Eliminate | Not Important | Interruptions Distractions Other Calls | Trivia Busy Work Time - Wasters | Minimise, Eliminate |

*Matrix courtesy of Wikimedia Creative Commons licence*

## Priorities in time order

There are only three categories of priority when you are a person on a mission:

*ACTION* – 'Do right away' and its subsets:
- 'Waiting for...
- The things you cannot do yet because of their dependencies on the actions of others; changes in, or clearer definition of regulations; arrival of skilled staff/ the right equipment; etc.
- Next bit
- Work one bite at a time.
- Matchmaking
- The sometimes-unlikely mix n' match required in times of crisis to get the job done effectively, if lacking in refinement.
- In due time
- The right order for maximum effectiveness.

*MAYBE* - If we have time and it makes sense to include and it doesn't need crutches or regular feeding – and its shape fits the way space/regulation/staffing is now configured. The old adage is important to remember:

*Your first answer is NO because it can be changed – unlike its counterpart YES.*

*STOP* – and its subsets:
- Rethink totally
- Which makes sense when, in the process of changing something, you find there are just too many things that need adjusting to achieve the end result – or the demands are so different that you can't retrofit.

- Fix the broken bits
- It can be quicker to do a bit of radical surgery to repair a non-performing bit of the product/service/way things need to be laid out, than to start afresh.
- Dispose of thoughtfully:
  *A*ll recycling should be done with careful prior thought. Don't disconnect anything from your operating model before making sure you have mapped all its connections and dependencies and that in that disconnection you don't suddenly have an influx of emergencies caused by 'unexpected consequences' that you should have expected if you'd planned beforehand, had a backup plan to reconnect if required – and made sure nothing was irretrievably lost in the process.

## Activities en route
### *Fixing flat tyres*

You need an emergency roadside crew who can respond to the unexpected service calls or even to anticipate them and remedy before your customers stumble because of them.

In his book 'Fanning the Flames', former Liverpool Station Commander Dave Fanning employed some advice he had been given by a seasoned Fire Chief. This advice came to mind when Dave and his unit were faced with devastation from a gas explosion that demolished three houses. Upon arrival at the scene there were people in their night attire desperately pulling at the rubble for survivors.

Once his crew left the fire engine, Dave locked the doors and surveyed the scene. His mentor had warned him that in such cases the public will tear you apart trying to get attention to one thing or another when you need to have a few moments of rapid assessment so you can plan.

Dave watched as people grabbed at his fire fighter's equipment and heard the screamed request of 'over here' from one place and then the same desperate call from another.

Having had the few moments of calm to assess the entirety of the scene, he was then able to effectively direct the emergency. This resulted in the miraculous rescue of a mother and newborn baby – baby first and finally on a second foray under precariously balanced debris, the mother, protected by a bed that had fallen above her – and both only slightly injured.

Lock your fire-engine door and take a calm look at the landscape as it sits under the impact of the changes you couldn't have anticipated.

Stop. Survey. Take a deep breath and then act.

You need to have someone or a team of 'someones' empowered to respond in just such a way.

The chances of your company exploding are greater in a crisis that has not a lot to do with your own actions. Responding thoughtfully and with knowledge of all resources to hand may be the dividing line between success and failure.

Discuss with your team who these 'someones' will be and make clear their boundaries in decision making.

## Going somewhere new

When travelling in the arctic, your compass isn't much use because of the capricious nature of magnetic north: it wanders.

Similarly, in life in the current fast-changing world the compass we have always used cannot be relied upon to produce results as effectively as it did when the landscape hadn't shifted.

This means that as you act on the results of your SWIVEL you need to keep making sure you are still on course. As we saw with the ill-fated Korean Airlines flight that wandered 180 nautical miles off course into missile launching airspace, such a mistake can get you shot down pretty fast if people mistake your intentions – or if you just find yourself unable to communicate effectively.

Where before we used "So what?", now we need to qualify our next planned activities with an equally important question:

*What could possibly go wrong?*

...and not in the joking manner we usually say when it is perfectly obvious what *can* go wrong.

Just like the pilots on that Korean Airlines flight who had no idea there was a problem, your situation may also not be obvious to you, so having a 'second guessing group' may not be a bad plan.

Give your usual 'Nay Sayers' a chance to have their head. These are the people who always can be relied upon to claim why anything won't work. Normally they are a burr under the saddle, but now is the time to employ their unique perspective and listen to what they have to say.

We are all so used to hearing the droning lists of gloom of such people, that they become 'white noise' – just part of the background hum we block out of our consciousness. This time listen carefully: what may be embedded within their observations might be the information you needed to change course slightly so you can navigate safely out of foreign airspace. As you proceed in that direction, it is also useful to remember the old adage:

*Sometimes, the quickest way through is around.*

### I spy with my little eye
It is also useful as you plan a route into unknown territory to remember that the route looks different going in different directions.

Remember how sometimes you have commented on this when travelling unfamiliar routes by car? This is because when a route is unfamiliar, you note all the small details that become just part of the scenery when you travel it often. Take the time to do just that.

Note all the details as you embark on your new path in both directions – another **Swivel**. Note in your book.

Remember the neuroscience that explains how create connections occur when hand-written? If you have your book with you all the time, jot as you go. It will prove invaluable. These notes may give you useful signals of unanticipated customer behavior or need. These are often small details that collectively build an informative picture – but won't if we don't prepare ourselves to watch for them and note them for wider assessment.

We find it useful to get people to also use some sort of have a central repository of where the hand-written notes are summarized onto some sort of dedicated whiteboard This way, as people pass and see something it can spark connection to something in *their* book as they notice something unexpected or just delightful – or cautionary.

We prefer a whiteboard in a route that is widely travelled by most of your team. If it is 'Up there' for people to see as they pass by, it may just cause dots to connect in different ways when it sparks a thought in a passer-by.

### *Picking up new passengers*

Allow for the opportunity to collaborate en route. You may discover that there is a company that provides a better service or part than that you are currently using – and that its incorporation would add value to your overall proposition. Don't defensively hold to the old one if the new will be an improvement.

Working on a global IT project that changed the workplace for all users of a major oil and gas company, a colleague of mine in Ireland discovered a company that had identified a major flaw in the overall reporting of the new workplace environment software and developed a whole company around just doing that bit exceptionally well.

Having just spent the equivalent of ten person-days in long hours in my hotel room in a foreign country taking out all the 'noise' that the flaw in the original caused, I was eager to evaluate.

This was not a trivial thing as I had to give a report to the Board of a major energy producer that the error reporting of the offending environment listed over 22,000 problems. When I laboriously examined every one (with lots of midnight oil and red wine), I was able to demonstrate that most of those 'errors' could be grouped under the following types of headings:

- Will automatically be corrected by the new software
- Functionality has been improved and the problem doesn't exist in the new environment
- Duplicate differently expressed

Ultimately, I was able to show that there were actually 26 issues and demonstrate how we would deal with each of them.

You would think that making the case for using the proprietary services of the specialist company who did for a living what I had just done would be a 'no-brainer' – but technical people in the corporation were awfully fond of fixing things and had worked out a circuitous – and not very effective – method of tinkering with the original component to give slightly less noise. It took the concerted efforts of my colleague in Ireland and me in Germany to finally make the case for NO 'noise'.

The ensuing collaboration with the specialist company resulted in considerable new business for us over the ensuing 12 months. That new business had a surprising element. We had recognised that with their process incorporated, our more streamlined reporting made a more attractive and convincing proposition but had not anticipated the leads the specialist company brought to us – leads that brought over 54 new contracts.

As you SWIVEL you are taking in a variety of perspectives of your 'property'.

In 'Previews and Premises[98]', author Alvin Toffler stated that property isn't what it used to be. He points out the difference between 'info-property' and 'real property.

'Info-property' is not finite; it can be used by many people at the same time and in doing so this often generates more info-property. Information is generative. Are there parts of your 'Info-property' that when shared would generate shared new profits?

Is there some part of what you are planning for the future that is not elegant within your own methods or product? Find who does nothing but that and therefore

[98] Previews and Premises, Alvin Toffler – My copy inherited from my Dad and printed in 1984

does it well – and offer them the opportunity for you to ride together into the complexity-filled, changeable future landscape.

### Stripping down – Reduce drag

When I was a teenager, my older brother had just developed what was to be a lifelong passion for rehabilitating antique and classic cars. We used to joke about the 'boy racers' and with disdain comment on their 'twin overhead foxtails' (as we called them – the imitation fox tails that used to fly from radio antennae). We sarcastically joked that these foxtails were obviously designed to produce extra speed – something their racing stripes painted on the side of their shiny, noisy vehicles would accelerate.

Such sarcasm might well be something you could apply to your own company.

Just as the boy racer foxtails would produce drag that would slow rather than increase speed; you may have some of your own that you think are pretty fancy but are actually slowing down your progress.

Take input from your teams. They may have been making similar observations as we did about the foxtails and racing stripes. Sometimes, using times of crisis to remove things that were slowing down your ability to be more efficient can be done without the usual 'fahldeerah' that would have otherwise erupted.

Take the opportunity to strip down while there is the lowest level of resistance. How to know what to strip, why and where? In 'The Laws of Simplicity', my version printed in 2006, author John Maeda gives us a good ruler by which to measure.

*How simple can you make it?*
*How complex does it have to be?*

As Peter Drucker writes in 'The Age of Discontinuity', (my version 1971):

*The most difficult ad most important decisions in respect to objectives are not what to do. They are, firstly, what to abandon as no longer worthwhile and secondly, what to give priority to, and what to concentrate on.*

Ed Morrison, the Founder of Strategic Doing has another piece of advice. The easiest first thing is to *stop doing stupid things*. The analogy he uses is:

*'Don't keep putting the shower curtain outside of the bath'*

### Alignment - 'Fit for Purpose' check

Please make a final safety check before you launch into this fast changing atmosphere of rapid and unpredictable change. Find what aviators called the 'Swiss Cheese' effect in your plans and stress to everyone the importance of their role in the checks they make to be sure your craft is airworthy before it takes flight. This suggests that you have identified the possible single points of failure in your forward plans and have taken thoughtful steps to be sure that they cannot occur.

Swiss cheese is what aviators describe after accidents caused by everyone in the chain of checking their particular part of the safety of things not doing their bit – all at the same time – hence lining up the holes in what was designed to be a Swiss Cheese that forgave one or perhaps even two holes aligning / aka errors.

When a vintage glider is restored and gets its airworthy certificate, the regulations in the UK require that the person issuing that certificate be the first to fly it. It's a great incentive for eliminating errors.

There may be elements of this principle that you may want to use in testing your new pathways to the post pandemic world.

### *White flags – collaborating where you used to compete*

What can you do with the companies that you thought were competitors that will result in better services or products – and will give better return for each of you?

In 'Management and Machiavelli' Antony Jay calls them parallel worlds that should be examined – but cautions that you find the right parallel worlds.

Chris Zook, in 'Unstoppable', gives us an example of a parallel world that still develops fortunes, after earlier being in bankruptcy that forced restructuring and suffering massive boardroom insurrection . From this emerged a gifted leader in Avi Arad. This is the story of Marvel. It is a story detailed on the *'denofgeek.com'* website (link in footnotes[99]) and has many lessons in its full history. Having relied upon the comic book market for too long, Marvel was faced with vastly diminished markets. In Arad's **Swivel**, he looked into two areas: core assets and a parallel world.

The *core asset* was the existence of more than 5,000 comic book characters that already had a devoted following. The *parallel world* was that of movies.

Marvel weren't satisfied with just one **Swivel**. The solution was waiting in the wings on their first swivel and on the next they expanded their parallel world when they swivelled again. When entering the parallel world of Hollywood proved too fraught with issues, Marvel brokered a deal with Merrill Lynch that gave it the financing to become an independent film-maker. This resulted in its much-loved comic characters becoming blockbuster movie stars : think 'Spider-Man' and 'The Hulk'. Then came another parallel world when Marvel was bought by Disney and went on to make 'The Avengers', 'Iron Man 3' and 'The Black Panther'.

As Sullivan and Harper write, in 'Hope is Not a Method', peripheral vision is a rare commodity – and just as rare in times of crisis. This book may widen yours.

> *The only thing worse than being blind*
> *is having sight but no vision.*
> Helen Keller

---

[99] https://www.denofgeek.com/movies/how-marvel-went-from-bankruptcy-to-billions/

# CHAPTER NINE
# Forward into the future

*The world makes way for the man*
*who knows where he is going.*

Ralph Waldo Emerson

**ACT**

### *Authenticity and reliability*

Do you have an integrated service or product line where each of its components reflects the same 'brand value'? Does every part of it reflect that key message?

On a different level: I recently ordered from another online company where I had never before shopped. It was a simple purchase: a frame for a photo to sit on the wall above my desk. I needed to have a coloured passepartout (a picture mount) cut to size because it wasn't a standard sized photo.

First pass: I ordered with measurements and then thought I had better employ the carpenter's rule and measure twice before having something cut. Returning to the site, the original order was not obvious, so I ordered with the corrected dimensions. A little while later I received two emails – oops. I had indeed ordered correctly *and* incorrectly.

I hastily sent a return email explaining and received a quick response cheerfully telling me not to worry – they would discard the incorrect one.

My parcel duly arrived with frame and perfectly dimensioned insert - plus a lovely postcard of three dogs of character sitting on the grass behind a picture frame *(probably photo-shopped)* across which was strung bunting with the letters spelling out 'Thank You' and a central one between the two words with a paw print.

The dogs were in costume and discarded bits of costume were strewn around beside them. The reverse side had all the helpful things about satisfaction and contact details and invitations to follow on social media – and at the bottom in small capital letters:

*No dogs have been harmed in the making of this card.*
*These are our own Frame Company[100] Doggies*
*and have been paid for their time with treats and love.*

Does such an investment pay off? Well it is here as an example - and is promoting their brand. It also endorses what Virginia Postrel writes in 'The Substance of Style' about how research has demonstrated that 'sensory pleasure works to commercial and personal advantage because *aesthetics* (my italics) has intrinsic value'.

---

[100] https://frame-company.co.uk/

Postrel goes on in another part of the book to explain that the purpose of 'aesthetics' is not to tell us what our purpose should be, for at most it just

*communicates something about what those purposes are, reminding ourselves and the world of what we think is important.'*

What are the aesthetics of your offer and what do they speak to? Do they that still have resonance in a world where values and relationships have been upended across the globe?

Your aesthetics are important for all the subliminal messages they send. Examine them for their fitness to your newly evaluated offerings to a more critical marketplace.

The Frame Company of this example is a small British firm – and they have made a lifelong customer of me – and employed me as their unpaid marketing representative. Their products are quality but not remarkable in a market of picture frames – but they have stamped their authenticity into the transaction – making it memorable and using a bit of fun to do so.

This is the 'You' we mentioned earlier that distinguishes one from another – but it is also a measure of authenticity – of caring that every element of the relationship is true to the values of the company.

In 'Overbooked', author Elizabeth Becker highlights the authenticity of her trip on the National Geographic's 'Sea Lion'. The crew are paid US level wages and compensation instead of lower wages that depend upon cabin tips – the model of most major cruise companies.

By contrast to the big cruise companies selling diamonds on board, National Geographic offers interaction at the visited location with people who really benefit from purchases of authentic goods at the local level - so profits don't travel back to corporate pockets. In short: a trip on 'Sea Lion' lives up to the expectation of tours under a trusted brand and their promise to protect integrity of place.

## Do you recognise me? Brand
The only reason to rebrand in a crisis is to be clearer to everyone what core business you are in. Rebranding done well takes time. You may not have the time right now to do it, so if you do there has to be a really good reason.

### *Rebranding: The FedEx effect*
In terms of the time it takes to rebrand, when Federal Express rebranded, they did so globally overnight on 24th June 1994.

Like most overnight successes, the transformation of the brand was the culmination of two years of research and testing. It was also a great case of getting it right the second time. The first change hadn't done the job.

For the two previous years they operated on an earlier rebrand from 'Federal Express' to 'FDX': doesn't quite roll off the tongue, does it?

*First the WHY?*

When formed, the company had effectively added leverage to the 'trust' value of the word 'Federal' and the 'trust' value of the livery of the US Postal service. This assisted in a new company securing contracts that were indeed Federal. But the value of an association with anything federal didn't have the same trust value in many of the new countries into which FedEx later expanded its business.

*Then the WHAT?*

The company had rethought the delivery business. Why not overnight delivery to meet the increasing speed of expanding business?

It was a unique concept at the time. Reputedly, it was so revolutionary that XEROX was distrustful of its ability to deliver the promise. Because of this distrust, for two weeks empty boxes from XEROX were shipped from here to there before the company entrusted physical content to this revolutionary system – because 'everyone knew it couldn't be done'. FedEx proved it could.

The company then did a further ***Swivel*** as they assessed the value they can add to the whole shipping experience by looking to its end-to-end needs. No longer a business sector that had held close to the business model of the Pony Express, shipment of packages had entered a totally new world full of demand that was becoming more sophisticated.

The rebrand saw new signs over the doors of the extended stabling of FedEx ponies: FedEx Freight; FedEx services (technology to manage supply chains, e-commerce etc); FedEx Office – (if you are in the US, think Kinkos on steroids) -and FedEx Logistics. The subliminal white space arrow between the Orange 'E' and lower case 'X' have added a story to the logo with its transcribed meaning of 'fast forward'.

In 2024, the stables were consolidated into Ground and Air services, with FedEx 'Less than a Load' group remaining a stand-alone group under the ground freight group.

If you totally rebrand, do so carefully.

### Polishing the brand
If you just rebrand in terms of relevance to the market of a changed world – without change to livery and logo and all that goes with it – and frankly, most companies haven't either the time or the resources to point in that direction – then what you need is a good car wash to put the sparkle where it will have the best effect.

Like any good car detailer you will look at all the tiny details that go with your brand and before polishing see if they are worth the effort or should be discretely disengaged and either sent to a recycler – someone who can do that bit of the business better than you, or else redesigned into something more useful for your offering.

Do the repairs needed quickly but with care and think through any unintended consequences. As we have said before – the folk at the pointy end of the ship may not be the right people to ask – go to the engine room and get them to check. Especially in the times that have erupted in global shift of relationships and possibilities – don't pay lip service. Don't even start to compose responses to sit within your brand until you have checked under the sofa for any 'headline-worthy errors of judgement' in your own company's past.

Be sure you have reached a point of no return on your statement of values – because believe me, you will be held to them.

Here is an example of brand polishing from Michael Gershman's book 'Getting it Right the Second Time'. We've talked about Jell-O before but this is an interesting way of marrying brand to perceived value so it is instantly memorable in that context.

In this case it was polishing the brand to marry it to the value of 'belonging'. Jell-O created a special series of recipe books in the different languages of immigrants of that time and gave it to them to help them feel 'at home' with one of America's most recognisable fun foods.

Have a look at your brand vs. what you now deliver. Do they match? If they do but there is room for improvement, do what it takes.

One chain of restaurants featuring only Italian food had expanded its menu so enthusiastically that people found it confusing and quality assurance was variable. A new CEO reduced the menu to what the brand originally stood for: good pasta, great sauces and good quality meat.

Southwest Airlines has been the poster child for matching its brand to the experience for decades. Their brand stands for an outstanding end-to-end experience'
A wonderful story repeated about Southwest on the blog *bombbomb.com*[101] gives this story.

On a Southwest flight the flight attendant announced that there was on board a young lady who was turning five years old today. She then explained that although they didn't have a cake for her to celebrate, if everyone to join in, they could help the young lady blow out her candles. She asked everyone to turn on their overhead reading lights and then dimmed the cabin lights. The little girl was then brought to the front of the cabin and told to blow out her candles. As she blew, every passenger in the whole aircraft turned off his or her light.

I recount another Southwest story in my book 'Shrapnel Free Explosive Growth'. It tells of how a last minute booking was made and a Granddaddy rushed to the airport after being told his grandson was about to be taken off life support in another city and he had hours to say his last goodbye.

The heavy peak hour traffic caused him to be delayed and he rushed to the departure gate where the flight had closed - only to find the Captain waiting for him. The man's wife had called to advise Southwest of the situation and beg them to wait.

---

[101] https://bombbomb.com/blog/the-customer-experience-podcast-kurt-bartolich/

The Captain told him not to rush any more. The plane wasn't going anywhere without him – and he wasn't going anywhere without Granddaddy. The Flight Attendants had advised the passengers of the reason for the delay and welcomed Granddaddy aboard with applause and kind gestures.

That means that Southwest missed their departure slot – something other airlines would not take lightly to because of the knock on effect and associated costs. It means that this is a company that supports even such an expensive decision because it is 'the right thing to do'.It also means that both flight attendant and Captain knew what their brand stood for and what they stood for on its behalf.

An important thing about these two stories is that they are not part of a company's advertising or promotion. Southwest didn't alert the world to them. They each came from a passenger on the flight where these examples of 'owning' the company took place.

Do your people have the empowerment to polish your brand and help your customers get a memorable experience by doing the 'little things' that endorse your brand?

That's one way to polish a brand. It may be your best.

## Creating fixers – Empowerment
### *Empowerment and responsibility*

On the point of empowerment, let's start out with the cautionary statement made in 'Hope is not a Method', by authors Sullivan and Harper:

*Empowerment is not about power.*
*It is about responsibility.*

John P. Kotter also wrote in 'A Force for Change: How leadership differs from Management' that setting direction and long-term planning are two very different things that should not be confused.

Setting direction is your job as leader. Kotter gives four components of making that leadership 'sticky'.

- Put the objective in terms of the values of your people so that it has personal relevance.
- Involve people in getting to work on the bits most relevant to them.
- Support those efforts enthusiastically and provide whatever coaching that is useful – not necessarily by you.
- Give public recognition for their efforts and achievements and reward accordingly.

In 'Thick Face, Black Heart', Chin-Ning Chu has another important caution.

*Beware the smallest.*

It is the small thing that can be the greatest destroyer of all your efforts. You will never find the small thing unless your people feel empowered to tell you bad news.

I recently heard a story that may just be urban myth but bears out my point. It goes like this:

In the former Soviet Union the person who brought the bad news gets shot.

A city-dwelling student sent to work on a collective farm was told to weed a field. Not knowing a weed from the desired crop, she dutifully removed the crop and left the weeds. No one reported it because the person who does, gets shot.

The weeds grew heartily under tender care and when it came time to crop the field they were duly harvested and shipped off to the factory. The harvesting crew could see the problem but didn't mention it, because the person who does, gets shot.

When the weeds arrived at the factory, no one mentioned it because the person who does would get shot.

If you have a similar environment it is no wonder no one has told you some of the things you are now observing on your **Swivel**. No one will bear the responsibility in case they get shot.

Changing that environment to one where there is shared responsibility for what you are trying to do is the only viable route forward at the best of times – and these are not the best of times, so that need is even more urgent.

## Spontaneity and intuition
In 'Blink', Gladwell gives three examples of effective decision-making under duress. One is of a remarkable marine General by the name of Van Riper, known in the field as 'Rip'. After a career of remarkably successful

leadership in Vietnam and other active zones, Rip was chosen to be the rogue leader in a very complex, important, and expensive War Games Exercise.

The story is riveting, but the short version is that the Blue Team used all the technologies and methodologies available to them, while the victorious Red Team anticipated this and employed other (often manual) tactics – like using lighting systems to send messages instead of communication devices capable of being immobilised by satellite interruption.

The decisions of their leader were made spontaneously – there is no time for laborious methodology or discussion in crisis.

What is interesting is that on a later visit to the New York Stock Exchange Trading Floor, Rip recognised the similarity in decision-making by people who were the antithesis of marines. Yet when placed (as he arranged for them to do) in tanks or on the simulated battlefield, they were extremely effective.

It was not just Rip who recognised this. When the two groups mingled socially at a cocktail party there was not one of the many small groups actively in conversation that did not include both marines and traders. The physical differences couldn't have been greater – yet they were what Rip described as 'soul mates'.

The third example is of Imrov acting. The very name suggest that in Improv 'it just happens'. However, Improv actors train on being able to improvise and have a series of base rules which give a loose structure, possibly the most important of which is that each actor must accept everything that happens to him or her.

In other words – like battle – you cannot change the reality of the duress under which you must perform. From these examples, Gladwell distils our valuable lesson to heed as we plan forward.

*Spontaneous decision making is not random.*

In an organisation facing the sorts of unanticipated impacts that are features of this shift in world order– there is no time for people to consult laboriously detailed rule books on how to resolve things that are upsetting your customers, or stopping your system from enabling you to get your products and services effectively to the market.

You may have to deploy the mechanisms of the past that don't rely on technology – and they certainly should be aware that this is an option

To allow that freedom to be spontaneous you also need to have these performances under base rules so that any judgement made has sufficient background information – so don't hoard it all – hence the value of the team *Swivel*.

Not all their decisions your 'Fixers' make will be the best – but they will be the best they can make with the information they have to hand, so must be permitted to err in judgement. However,  if you are going to allow spontaneous decision making you also need to have made clear what I call the 'Rule of the Boundary Fence'. If everyone knows where the fence lies they won't go beyond it.

*The 'boundary fence' is defined by a common understanding of the points of failure that will bring the whole show to a grinding halt.*

It is worth investing a little of your precious limited time in establishing where your boundary fence lies and making sure that it is a clearly understood limitation of the area within which empowerment lies.

In 'Thinking Fast and Slow'[102], my version printed in 2011, author Daniel Kahneman gives an example similar to those of former Fire Fighting Station Commander Dave Fanning in his book 'Fanning the Flames'.

Kahneman tells of the Fire Ground Commander who was standing with other firefighters in a house when he suddenly yelled for everyone to evacuate immediately. They dashed out, just as the floor on which they had been standing collapsed.

He knew the danger intuitively – without knowing.

In later analysis it was that his ears were suddenly unusually hot and it was unusually quiet. Intuitively he knew that meant the fire was below them, not above. It is a classic case of 'Blink'.

---

[102] Thinking Fast and Slow', Daniel Kahneman – My copy printed in 2011

Kahneman is a bit of a Maven too – a collector of useful bits of information. In his own book he quotes from 'Blink' and also from Gary Klein's book 'Sources of Power' which again quotes from Herbert Simon who wrote in 1982 that rationality is bounded by the (my italics) *limits of our thinking capacity, availability of information, and time.*

Simon defined intuition this way:

*The situation has provided a cue;*
*this cue has given the expert*
*access to information stored in memory,*
*and (that) information provides the answer.*

*Intuition is nothing more or less than recognition.*

As you and your team **Assess** and before they **Act**, ask them all - and yourself - to note down things their intuition flags to them in the process of your ***Swivel***.

It is these 'small things' that can put patches in place before something goes bust – or suggest a re-route that bypasses looming hazards – or alerts you of trends or needs in the market of this new landscape (that they have 'whiffed) that would otherwise have bitten you in the ankle when they arrived.

In 'The Anatomy of Change[103], author Don Fabun makes a very important point that has relevance in the

---

[103] The Anatomy of Change , Don Fabun  - My copy from my Dad's library was printed in 1967

context of your 'Fixers' and their empowerment to act on behalf of the organisation. That point is that

*in most cases where change is needed,*
*it is not the world that has changed*
*– it is our experience of it that has.*

In our case – the world has changed in many ways but it is our experience of the change that we have to deal with. But it is also our ability to experience it that has changed as well - we have limited exposure to be in a position to have made that 'experience' when we are emerging from a more or less stable world of international relationships and trust. Fabun goes on to differentiate between two orders of change that have relevance for us as we plan our company future because we are experiencing both orders of change together.

*One type of change* is from a force that displaces things – and in this case, our experience of change is the way things have been displaced in time and space from their previous arrangements. These changes can be measured – and we will see many such measurements as a result of the changes of this global instability.

*The second order of change* is about the configuration of things and how they do not now relate to each other in the same way as before. In a social and cultural order of change, measurements are about quality, not quantity as in the first order of change.

Faber quotes Eric Hoffer, an American of parents from Alsace, who through his writings became an outspoken social commentator of the role of the under-classes which he once wrote were 'lumpy with talent'. His most famous book 'The True Believer' examines the emergence of mass movements as they arise from the frustrations of the populace and in that context he writes:

*It needs inordinate self confidence*
*to face drastic change without inner trembling.*

I trust that this book eases the trembling and your **Swivel** approach helps guide you to develop together a company that is truly 'anti-fragile' and grows positively through the impact of crisis.

Remember that I am a Maven, and a willing extra to your unpaid marketing team. Do let me know of your progress at www.archerbg.com.

*Warp speed, Mr. Sulu.*
*First star on the left, then straight on 'til morning.*

Captain Kirk of the Starship Enterprise

## The Four Questions and 10 Rules of Strategic Doing

## Before you Begin

1. Create a safe space for deep, focused conversations.

2. Frame the conversation around an appreciate question.

## What could we do?

3. Uncover hidden assets that people are willing to share.

4. Link & Leverage your assets to create new opportunities.

## What should we do?

5. Rank all your opportunities to find your "Big Easy".

6. Convert your Big Easy into an outcome with measurable characteristics.

## What will we do?

7. Define a Pathfinder Project with guideposts.

8. Create a short-term action plan with everyone taking a small step.

## What's our 30/30?

9. Set a next meeting to review progress and make adjustments.

10. Nudge, connect, and promote relentlessly to reinforce your new habits of collaboration.

# ANNEXE Source Books

These are the 63 books from which I drew direct analogies, ideas, quotations, and perspectives in my Swivel to develop a handbook for going into a future we cannot yet fully envisage.

Each lives in my library and perhaps has wider usefulness to your company than that which I have extracted for this book.

What I find truly amazing is how often and how precisely many of these authors warned of the events that we have unfolding in a radically changed world order. The necessity to change the value system has been clearly heralded.

The impacts on business, our communities and on our very lifestyles have been clearly stated. Our unwillingness to head cautions found in these books that were published as far back as 1958 has finally caught up with the world at its most vulnerable moments.

As we go forward in our company plan for a radically changed world order, we do well to factor into it the warning of Nassim Nicholas Taleb in 'Fooled by Randomness':

*It doesn't matter how frequently something succeeds if failure is too costly to bear.*

# INDEX

# INDEX

# INDEX

# INDEX

# INDEX

# INDEX

A helpful sign for your door as you Swivel *Again*

I am under construction

Thank you for your patience